**New Directions for
Community Colleges**

Arthur M. Cohen
EDITOR-IN-CHIEF

Richard L. Wagoner
ASSOCIATE EDITOR

Allison Kanny
MANAGING EDITOR

Applied and Workforce Baccalaureates

Deborah L. Floyd
Rivka A. Felsher
and Angela M.
Garcia Falconetti
EDITORS

Number 158 • Summer 2012
Jossey-Bass
San Francisco

APPLIED AND WORKFORCE BACCALAUREATES
Deborah L. Floyd, Rivka A. Felsher, and Angela M. Garcia Falconetti (eds.)
New Directions for Community Colleges, no. 158

Arthur M. Cohen, Editor-in-Chief
Richard L. Wagoner, Associate Editor
Allison Kanny, Managing Editor

NEW DIRECTIONS FOR COMMUNITY COLLEGES (ISSN 0194-3081, electronic ISSN 1536-0733) is part of The Jossey-Bass Higher and Adult Education Series and is published quarterly by Wiley Subscription Services, Inc., A Wiley Company, at Jossey-Bass, One Montgomery St., Ste. 1200, San Francisco, CA 94104. Periodicals Postage Paid at San Francisco, California, and at additional mailing offices. POSTMASTER: Send address changes to New Directions for Community Colleges, Jossey-Bass, One Montgomery St., Ste. 1200, San Francisco, CA 94104.

SUBSCRIPTIONS cost $89.00 for individuals and $275.00 for institutions, agencies, and libraries in the United States. Prices subject to change.

EDITORIAL CORRESPONDENCE should be sent to the Editor-in-Chief, Arthur M. Cohen, at the Graduate School of Education and Information Studies, University of California, Box 951521, Los Angeles, CA 90095-1521. All manuscripts receive anonymous reviews by external referees.

New Directions for Community Colleges is indexed in CIJE: Current Index to Journals in Education (ERIC), Contents Pages in Education (T&F), Current Abstracts (EBSCO), Ed/Net (Simpson Communications), Education Index/Abstracts (H. W. Wilson), Educational Research Abstracts Online (T&F), ERIC Database (Education Resources Information Center), and Resources in Education (ERIC).

Microfilm copies of issues and articles are available in 16mm and 35mm, as well as microfiche in 105mm, through University Microfilms Inc., 300 North Zeeb Road, Ann Arbor, MI 48106-1346.

CONTENTS

EDITORS' NOTES   1
Deborah L. Floyd, Rivka A. Felsher, Angela M. Garcia Falconetti

1. Applied and Workforce Baccalaureate Models   5
Deborah L. Floyd, Angela M. Garcia Falconetti, Rivka A. Felsher
This chapter presents models and terminology defining applied and
workforce baccalaureates.

2. Articulation to and from the Applied Associate Degree: 13
Challenges and Opportunities
Jan M. Ignash
This chapter identifies the opportunities and challenges presented in
articulating associate degree programs with applied and workforce
baccalaureates.

3. Washington State's Model and Programs: Applied Baccalau-   25
reate Degrees at Community and Technical Colleges
Christy England-Siegerdt, Michelle Andreas
This chapter describes the development and current status of applied
baccalaureate degrees in the state of Washington.

4. The Evolution of Workforce Baccalaureate Degrees in Florida   35
Judith Bilsky, Ian Neuhard, Mary G. Locke
This chapter highlights the history of workforce baccalaureate degrees
in Florida, documents the growth of these programs across the state,
and provides a framework for the designation of various degree types
and academic requirements.

5. The Applied and Workforce Baccalaureate at South Texas   47
College: Specialized Workforce Development Addressing
Economic Development
Juan E. Mejia
The impact of two bachelor of applied technology degrees of South
Texas College on higher education access for predominately Hispanic
students serves as an example of how such degrees increase participa-
tion rates for minority students.

6. The Work Experience Component of an Ontario College   57
Baccalaureate Program
Marguerite M. Donohue, Michael L. Skolnik
This chapter describes the results of case study research on the transfer
of learning from the classroom to the cooperative education workplace
and includes recommendations for curriculum changes to improve the
transfer of learning.

7. Why Applied Baccalaureates Appeal to Working Adults: 73
From National Results to Promising Practices
Debra Bragg, Collin Ruud
This chapter presents lessons learned from a national study of adult
learner enrollment in applied baccalaureate programs.

8. Institutional Challenges of Applied and Workforce Bacca-   87
laureate Programs
Richard L. Wagoner, Carlos Ayon
This chapter presents some of the challenges to the mission of the
community college that critics of the applied and workforce baccalaureates assert.

9. Graduate Education Issues and Challenges: Community   95
College Applied and Workforce Baccalaureates
Deborah L. Floyd, Rivka A. Felsher, Linda Catullo
This chapter discusses the articulation of community college applied
and workforce baccalaureates to graduate education.

INDEX   103

EDITORS' NOTES

The role of U.S. community colleges is expanding, as demonstrated by the emergence of community colleges offering their own baccalaureate degrees. The rationale often cited for these new degrees is that they are applied and workforce in nature and are designed in response to local, statewide, and national workforce needs and demands. Community colleges across the country are reexamining institutional missions to ensure the preservation of the original community college mission of access and affordability while serving as baccalaureate degree granting institutions.

Proponents of community college applied and workforce baccalaureates argue that the rationale for offering such degrees is to provide geographical, programmatic, and financial access to a baccalaureate-level education, leading to gainful and satisfying employment. Thus to many, applied and workforce baccalaureates serve as an extension of the community college mission of serving the citizenry. While proponents believe that offering these technical degrees is part of the evolution of community colleges, critics argue that the degrees are counter to the true mission of community colleges and thus, this movement is more revolutionary in nature. Critics are concerned with the impact of the community college baccalaureate degree as a challenge to the core mission of community colleges. While exceptions may be noted, most community college baccalaureate degrees offered to date are applied in nature and focus on workforce needs, thus building on the comprehensive community college mission.

Are applied and workforce baccalaureate degrees offered by community colleges a natural extension of their mission to provide relevant educational programs to their constituents? Or is this emerging emphasis on offering baccalaureate degrees a radical deviation from the tried-and-true mission of comprehensive community colleges? In short, is this movement more evolutionary or revolutionary? This *New Directions for Community Colleges* issue does not take sides on this controversial issue, but adds to the debate by providing a deeper understanding of this movement from the perspective of practitioners and scholars alike. The opportunities and challenges associated with offering these new baccalaureate degrees is illustrated with institutional examples.

This issue of *New Directions for Community Colleges* focuses on the most prevalent type of community college baccalaureate degree—applied and workforce baccalaureates. Applied baccalaureate degrees will include a blend of degrees as defined by Bragg and Ruud (2009), Floyd, Skolnik, and Walker (2005), Floyd and Walker (2009). Applied baccalaureate degrees often articulate with associate of applied science degrees in specialized

New Directions for Community Colleges, no. 158, Summer 2012 © 2012 Wiley Periodicals, Inc.
Published online in Wiley Online Library (wileyonlinelibrary.com) • DOI: 10.1002/cc.20011

1

fields such as technology management, business management, certain health professions, and information technology (Townsend, Bragg, & Ruud, 2009). Similarly, workforce baccalaureates are defined by Floyd and Walker (2009) as degrees that meet workforce demands and are offered for that specific purpose. Examples of fields of service for graduates of workforce baccalaureates include education, allied health, law enforcement, and public service, but they may also include fields such as biology if the college is offering the degree to fill a specific community workforce need. The terms "*applied*" and "*workforce*" are often used synonymously. Some states, such as Florida, for example, stipulate the requirement that these degrees meet local workforce needs.

Townsend, Bragg and Ruud's (2009) definition of applied baccalaureates differs from Floyd, Skolnik, and Walker's (2005) in that disciplines of teacher education and nursing are excluded in their research. Townsend, Bragg and Ruud's (2009) research, sponsored by the Lumina Foundation, includes a study of applied baccalaureates in universities and community colleges with a focus on adult learners. They posited that degrees in disciplines, such as nursing and teacher education, are not built upon applied courses, do not permit articulation with applied associate degrees, and are mostly offered by traditional four-year institutions. Concomitantly, Floyd and Walker's (2009) definition of workforce baccalaureates, as cited above, includes nursing and teacher education and notes that such degrees are created by traditional four-year institutions and community colleges to meet local workforce demands.

For our purposes, we are using a combined definition that incorporates the concepts of both applied and workforce baccalaureates offered by community colleges, including some institutions that have recently converted to baccalaureate colleges or state colleges. This broader definition includes a wider range of disciplines such as teacher education, nursing, technology management, business management, health professions, information and engineering technology, business management, allied health programs, law enforcement, and public service. All disciplines have one key link that ties them together—they were designed to meet identifiable workforce needs.

We believe that it is critical, with almost twenty states offering such degrees at this point in history, for *New Directions for Community Colleges* to address the trends and policy issues associated with applied and workforce baccalaureates. This *New Directions for Community Colleges* is the first volume dedicated to the community college baccalaureate (CCB) and specifically, the applied and workforce baccalaureate (AWB).

This issue spotlights manuscripts from scholars and practitioners in an effort to describe the CCB movement through research analyses and findings, while challenging readers to examine the implications for future research and practice. Deborah L. Floyd, Angela M. Garcia Falconetti, and Rivka A. Felsher in Chapter One address applied and workforce baccalaureate models and the impact of such models on the future state of higher education. The models serve as a foundation for understanding the diverse nature of the applied and workforce baccalaureate as points of access to upper level study for students.

Jan M. Ignash authored Chapter Two, identifying the opportunities and challenges presented in articulating associate degree programs with applied and workforce baccalaureates with a focus on the state of Washington. The transfer of academic programs and credit between associate degrees and applied and workforce baccalaureates is examined as a means for further understanding the diversity of this phenomenon between postsecondary institutions.

Christy England-Siegerdt and Michelle Andreas, in Chapter Three, describe the development and current status of applied baccalaureate degrees also in the state of Washington. Comparatively, in Chapter Four, Judith Bilsky, Ian Neuhard, and Mary G. Locke describe the history of workforce baccalaureate degrees in Florida, document the growth of these programs across the state, and provide a framework for the designation of various degree types and academic requirements.

Juan E. Mejia, in Chapter Five, highlights the evolution of South Texas College in offering two bachelor's degrees and the impact of the degrees on increasing graduation rates of Hispanic students. In Chapter Six, Marguerite M. Donohue and Michael L. Skolnik describe the results of a case study regarding the transfer of learning in a baccalaureate program in a community college in Ontario, Canada. The chapter also focuses on the role of the work experience component of the program.

Debra Bragg and Collin Ruud, in Chapter Seven, present lessons learned from a national study of adult learner enrollment in applied baccalaureate programs. Bragg and Ruud also detail several baccalaureate models, such as upside-down, super-technical, and managerial. In Chapter Eight, Richard L. Wagoner and Carlos Ayon discuss the challenges to the community college mission posed by the applied and workforce baccalaureate. Lastly, Deborah L. Floyd, Rivka A. Felsher, and Linda Catullo in Chapter Nine, raise issues about the articulation of graduates from applied and workforce baccalaureate programs to graduate programs.

This volume on applied and workforce baccalaureates emphasizes the complex and sometimes controversial nature of community colleges as major stockholders of baccalaureate education. The distinguished authors of this issue intend for research findings on the applied and workforce baccalaureate to serve as resources for policy leaders, practitioners, and researchers who wish to further examine the emerging trend not only in the United States, but also internationally.

References

Townsend, B., Bragg, D., and Ruud, C. M. "Development of the Applied Baccalaureate." *Community College Journal of Research and Practice*, 2009, 33(9), 686–705.

Floyd, D. L., Skolnik, M., and Walker, K. P. (Eds.). *Community College Baccalaureate: Emerging Trends and Policy Issues*. Sterling, VA.: Stylus Publishing, 2005.

Floyd, D. L., and Walker, K. P. "The Community College Baccalaureate: Putting the Pieces Together." *Community College Journal of Research and Practice*, 2009, 33(2), 90–124.

DEBORAH L. FLOYD *is a professor and the program leader of higher education leadership at Florida Atlantic University.*

RIVKA A. FELSHER *is a doctoral candidate of higher education leadership at Florida Atlantic University.*

ANGELA M. GARCIA FALCONETTI *is the vice president of institutional advancement at Virginia Western Community College.*

NEW DIRECTIONS FOR COMMUNITY COLLEGES • DOI: 10.1002/cc

1

This chapter presents models and terminology representative of the contemporary utilization of the terms community college baccalaureate, applied baccalaureate, *and* workforce baccalaureate *to provide a foundation for the evolving language about pathways leading to baccalaureate degrees.*

Applied and Workforce Baccalaureate Models

Deborah L. Floyd, Angela M. Garcia Falconetti, Rivka A. Felsher

Community colleges have a storied history of successfully providing pathways and access to credentials and degrees through various models of delivery and in diverse programs of study. Until recently, the highest degree offered by community colleges was the associate degree. During the past decade, major changes have occurred in the landscape of higher education, with one of the most significant being the expansion of community college missions to include the delivery and conferring of baccalaureate degrees.

The community college baccalaureate has emerged as a continued pathway to a higher level of education—four-year degrees with specializations in applied and workforce fields of study, such as technology, management, business, nursing, engineering, and teacher education. As community colleges evolved from junior colleges to comprehensive institutions, contemporary community colleges demonstrated a commitment to increased access to the baccalaureate through education partnerships. Providing access to baccalaureate degree credentials is not new for community colleges, as almost all implement some form of partnerships. Such partnership models include *articulation models, university extension models, university center models,* and *community college baccalaureate models* (Floyd, 2006; Floyd, 2005).

This chapter describes the aforementioned community college models and selected terminology as a means for further understanding the uses of the terms *community college baccalaureate, applied baccalaureate,* and *workforce baccalaureate.*

New Directions for Community Colleges, no. 158, Summer 2012 © 2012 Wiley Periodicals, Inc.
Published online in Wiley Online Library (wileyonlinelibrary.com) • DOI: 10.1002/cc.20012

Articulation Models

Most community colleges across the United States have articulation agreements with universities to ensure the effective and efficient transfer of community college associate degrees to university baccalaureates. Articulation agreements are the state, local, and institutional policies and principles that align the exit requirements of a community college with the receiving institution's baccalaureate or graduate programs of study (Falconetti, 2009). These agreements are fundamental to state higher education policy and are integral to the success or failure of many dimensions of higher education including access, equity, affordability, and degree productivity (Ignash and Townsend 2000, 2001; Wellman, 2002, 2007).

States such as Florida, Texas, Illinois, New York, California, Oklahoma, Tennessee, and Washington possess a transfer student rate above the national average as a result of formal collaboration between community colleges and universities (Floyd, 2006; Wellman, 2007). For example, Florida's 2+2 statewide articulation policy guarantees the students of the Florida College System enrollment at four-year public universities. The statewide 2+2 articulation policy is supported by a common course numbering system that aligns all courses of similar content offered at public community colleges and universities. Strong 2+2 systems, like Florida's, are well-coordinated and well-supported statewide policies that are geared to ensure the efficient and effective transfer of community college students to universities. Hence, access to a baccalaureate-level education is stipulated by statute and applicable to the twenty-eight colleges of the Florida College System and the eleven universities of the State University System.

University Centers and Concurrent-Use Campus Models

University centers and concurrent-use campuses are becoming more prevalent across the United States. Windham, Perkins, and Rogers noted that Wisconsin, Utah, and Texas operated with the most partnership campuses in the United States, followed by Kentucky, Oklahoma, Mississippi, and Virginia (Windham, Perkins, and Rogers, 2001). Lorenzo (2005) described six models of university center and concurrent-use partnerships: the *co-location* model, the *enterprise* model, the *integrated* model, the *virtual* model, the *sponsorship* model, and the *hybrid* model. All models presented by Lorenzo designated senior institutions or universities to confer the degree, as opposed to community colleges.

The *co-location* university center and concurrent-use model is defined by the use of space shared by the senior institution or university and community college. The *enterprise* model includes the use of a higher education center through which baccalaureate education partnerships are employed between community colleges and senior institutions and universities. Much like the *enterprise* model, the *integrated* model also includes the use of a higher education center to provide baccalaureate partnerships; however, the center is located on community college campuses. The *virtual* model solely encompasses the offering of upper level course work online, per distance education. The *sponsorship* model is defined by the community college operating a university center and determining baccalaureate curricular offerings. The *hybrid* model is comprised of the offering of baccalaureates by community colleges and partnering with the senior institutions or universities for other degrees, such as graduate programs (Lorenzo, 2005).

Community College Baccalaureate

The term *community college baccalaureate* (CCB) has been used to describe both degrees offered by community colleges in partnership with other institutions of higher education and those offered by colleges viewed as community colleges. Colleges with seamless articulation agreements that ensure students completing an associate degree will move to baccalaureate degree completion with ease may view this model as offering a "community college baccalaureate." Similarly, community colleges providing space on campus through university centers and other partnerships are offering "community college baccalaureate" degrees (Floyd and Walker, 2009). Most of the time, however, the term has been used to describe baccalaureate degrees conferred by community colleges on their campuses that added these degrees to their offerings while maintaining the community college mission of open access.

Community College Applied and Workforce Baccalaureate Models

Community college applied and workforce baccalaureate models include the offering of baccalaureates by community colleges in which the curriculum focuses on applied and workforce specializations and primarily articulates with associate in science degrees. The terms *applied* and *workforce* are often used interchangeably, as workforce degrees are generally in applied fields such as business, education, and nursing.

Townsend, Bragg, and Ruud's (2009) research includes a study of adult learners enrolled in applied baccalaureates in universities and community colleges (Ruud, Bragg, and Townsend, 2010). They posited that degrees in disciplines, such as nursing and teacher education, are not always built upon applied courses. Hence, such degrees do not easily lend themselves to the articulation of applied associate degrees. In contrast, Floyd and Walker (2009) and Floyd (2005) included teacher education, nursing, technology management, business management, and information technology in their definitions of applied and workforce baccalaureates. Furthermore, Floyd and Walker (2009) noted that degrees such as nursing

NEW DIRECTIONS FOR COMMUNITY COLLEGES • DOI: 10.1002/cc

and teacher education that are created by four-year universities do in fact articulate with applied science degrees.

Determining how many CCBs exist is literally trying to hit a moving target. The American Association of State Colleges and Universities (AASCU) documented 465 CCB programs at fifty-four institutions in eighteen states in October of 2010 (Russell, 2010). These figures are already out of date as new CCB programs come online across the nation each semester. The growth of the CCB is truly exponential. However, Florida has led the nation in the number of community colleges authorized to offer baccalaureate degrees. Initially intended to provide a means for increasing the workforce in areas such as teaching and nursing, Florida expanded its reach to include degrees such as interior design and engineering technology.

Florida's oldest community college, St. Petersburg College, was the first in the state approved to offer baccalaureates. In 2001, Florida enacted Senate Bill No. 1162, which granted St. Petersburg College the authority to confer baccalaureate degrees in content areas that specifically addressed the workforce demands of private and public employers such as nursing, teacher education, and information technology (Floyd and Falconetti, in press; Smith and Holcombe, 2008). The CCB has since expanded significantly in Florida in the last decade. As of June 2012, the colleges of the Florida College System offer approximately 145 applied and workforce baccalaureates (Florida Department of Education, 2012b). According to the Florida Department of Education, 19,266 students were enrolled in a CCB program in 2010–2011, with 2,729 achieving their dream of graduating with their baccalaureate from a community college (Florida Department of Education, 2012a).

Types of Applied and Workforce Baccalaureates

Ignash and Kotun (2005) posited that regardless of the method in which applied and workforce baccalaureates are offered, such degrees can be categorized into three types: *career ladder*, *inverse* or *upside-down*, and *management ladder degrees*. The *career ladder* applied and workforce baccalaureate program requires the majority of upper-level courses to focus on the technical major of the applied baccalaureate. For example, Florida State College at Jacksonville, in Jacksonville, Florida, offers a bachelor of applied science (B.A.S.) in Fire Science. The principal admission requirement for the B.A.S. is the completion of an associate in science (A.S.) in fire science technology (Florida State College at Jacksonville, 2011). The A.S. and B.A.S. degrees are based on the recommended core curriculum of the National Fire Academy, which emphasizes the advancement of fire science, administrative management skills, and critical communication skills (Florida State College at Jacksonville, 2011).

The *inverse* or *upside-down* applied and workforce baccalaureate includes the bachelor of applied studies (B.A.S.), the bachelor of general studies (B.G.S.), and the bachelor of professional studies (B.P.S.). The B.A.S., B.G.S., and B.P.S. turn the traditional curriculum sequence of general studies pursued during the associate degree upside down by accepting courses in the associate degree that satisfy the specific content-area curriculum requirements of the baccalaureate. Additional general education courses are completed during the pursuit of upper level study. In cases where the B.G.S. articulates solely with applied associate degree courses, Ignash and Kotun (2005) classified it as an upside-down applied baccalaureate. Townsend, Bragg, and Ruud (2009) cite New Mexico State University's B.A.S. degree that is offered through the College of Extended Learning to students possessing A.A.S. degrees as an upside-down applied CCB because that particular B.A.S. degree includes a curriculum that is broader in nature.

The *management ladder* applied and workforce baccalaureate offers a curriculum that prepares students with applied management skills sufficient to operate effectively in a managerial role. For example, several of the colleges of Florida's College System, such as Daytona State College and Brevard State College, offer B.A.S. degrees in supervision and management. Such B.A.S. degrees are offered by colleges of business, preparing students to work effectively and efficiently in managerial and supervisory roles. The degrees include courses such as management, leadership, and business fundamentals.

Looking to the Future

Community colleges across the United States have forged critical partnerships to provide students with access to the baccalaureate. Such baccalaureate pathway models as *articulation, university extension, university center,* and *community college baccalaureate* models present the applied and workforce baccalaureate in various forms to meet the access needs of students. The types of applied and workforce baccalaureate models as categorized by Ignash and Kotun (2005), *career ladder, inverse* or *upside-down,* and *management ladder degrees,* further develop Floyd and others' (2005; 2006) models of degree provision.

As new models emerge for providing access to students and directly delivering baccalaureate degrees by community colleges and partners, new terms and models will continue to develop. Evolutionary change is often messy, and terminology for research purposes often does not reflect practicing models until many years after implementation. Nevertheless, continuing efforts should be made to sort and classify delivery models for purposes of understanding and research, especially for measures of effectiveness and for policy making and funding considerations.

If the past is a predictor of the future, more states will join this movement by authorizing community colleges to offer baccalaureate degrees, especially in high-need areas to meet local workforce demands. Universities and other providers of baccalaureate degrees will decrease their emphasis on certain baccalaureate degrees offered by community colleges and focus more on specialized, research-based, and scholarly fields, as well as graduate education. College missions, and even names, will continue to change to more accurately describe their evolution. State systems will also evolve, as Florida did when the system name was changed to the Florida College System and many institutions changed their names from *community college* to *state college*.

While traditionalists view these changes as revolutionary, others see this as a time of evolutionary change. As universities evolved and elevated priorities such as graduate education and research, community colleges stepped forward to fill the gaps and address unmet needs. Individually and with partners, community colleges continue to address unmet needs and develop new pathways, new models, and creative new terminology to deliver viable baccalaureate degrees in formats that are relevant, accessible, and affordable. We enter a new era as community colleges evolve and creatively address new challenges and opportunities.

References

Falconetti, A. M. G. "The Perceived Effects of State Governance Decentralization on Baccalaureate Articulation." *Community College Journal of Research and Practice*, 2009, 33(2), 177–194.

Florida Department of Education. College Facts at a Glance. Florida Department of Education, 2012a, at http://www.fldoe.org/cc/facts_glance.asp

Florida Department of Education. Florida Colleges: Bachelor's Degree Programs. Florida Department of Education, 2012b, at http://www.fldoe.org/cc/students/bach_degree.asp

Florida State College at Jacksonville. "Fire Science Management." *Florida State College Catalog*, 2011, at floridastatecollegecatalog.fscj.edu/preview_program.php?catoid=18&poid=3917

Floyd, D. L. "Community College Baccalaureate in the U.S.: Models, Programs, and Issues." In D. L. Floyd, M. L. Skolnik, and K. P. Walker (eds.), *Community College Baccalaureate: Emerging Trends and Policy Issues*. Sterling, VA.: Stylus Publishing, 2005.

Floyd, D. L. "Achieving the Baccalaureate through the Community College." In D. D. Bragg and E. A. Barnett (eds.), *Special Issue: Academic Pathways to and from the Community College*. New Directions for Community Colleges, no. 135. San Francisco: Jossey-Bass, 2006.

Floyd, D. L., and Falconetti, A. "The Community College Baccalaureate Movement in Florida: A Decade of Change." In R. Remington and N. Remington (eds.), *Alternative Pathways to the Baccalaureate*. Sterling, VA.: Stylus Publishing, in press.

Floyd, D. L., and Walker, K. P. "The Community College Baccalaureate: Putting the Pieces Together." *Community College Journal of Research and Practice*, 2009, 33(2), 90–124.

Ignash, J., and Kotun, D. "Results of a National Study of Transfer in Occupational Technical Degrees: Policies and Practices." *Journal of Applied Research in the Community College*, 2005, 12(2), 109–120.

Ignash, J., and Townsend, B. K. "Evaluating Statewide Articulation Agreements According to Practice." *Community College Review*, 2000, 28(3), 1–21.

Ignash, J., and Townsend, B. K. "Statewide Transfer and Articulation Policies: Current Practices and Emerging Issues." In B. K. Townsend and S. B. Twombly (eds.), *Community Colleges* (pp. 173–192). Westport, CT: Albex, 2001.

Lorenzo, A. L. "The University Center: A Collaborative Approach to Baccalaureate Degrees." In D. L. Floyd, M. L. Skolnik, and K. P. Walker (eds.), *Community College Baccalaureate: Emerging Trends and Policy Issues* (pp. 73–93). Sterling, VA.: Stylus Publishing, 2005.

Russell, A. "Update on the Community College Baccalaureate: Evolving Trends and Issues." *Policy Matters: A Higher Education Policy Brief*, American Association of State Colleges and Universities, Washington, DC, October 2010, at http://www.aascu.org/uploadedFiles/AASCU/Content/Root/PolicyAndAdvocacy/PolicyPublications/AASCU_Update_Community_College_Baccalaureate(1).pdf

Ruud, C. M., Bragg, D., and Townsend, B. "The Applied Baccalaureate Degree: The Right Time and Place." *Community College Journal of Research and Practice*, 2010, 34(1), 136–152.

SB 1162, Florida Legislature Regular Session, 2001.

Smith, E. J., and Holcombe, W. "Baccalaureate Programs in Community Colleges." Tallahassee, FL.: Florida Department of Education, 2008.

Townsend, B., Bragg, D., and Ruud, C. M. "Development of the Applied Baccalaureate." *Community College Journal of Research and Practice*, 2009, 33(9), 686–705.

Wellman, J. V. State Policy and Community College-Baccalaureate Transfer. San Jose, C.A.: National Center of Public Policy and Higher Education and the Institute for Higher Education Policy, 2002, at www.highereducation.org/reports/transfer/transfer.shtml.

Wellman, J. V. "Policy Alert: Summary of State Policy and Community College Baccalaureate Transfer." San Jose, CA.: The National Center of Public Policy and Higher Education, 2007.

Windham, P., Perkins, G. R., and Rogers, J. "Concurrent-Use Programs: Part of the New Definition of Access." *Community College Review*, 2001, 29(3), 39–55.

DEBORAH L. FLOYD *is a professor and the program leader of higher education leadership at Florida Atlantic University.*

ANGELA M. GARCIA FALCONETTI *is the vice president of institutional advancement at Virginia Western Community College.*

RIVKA A. FELSHER *is a doctoral candidate of higher education leadership at Florida Atlantic University.*

NEW DIRECTIONS FOR COMMUNITY COLLEGES • DOI: 10.1002/cc

2

This chapter discusses the "tangled knot" of articulating associate degrees in applied fields and reviews sample programs from applied associate (A.A.S.) to baccalaureate degrees using three distinct pathways, comparing the resulting A.A.S. to baccalaureate degree pathways to similar B.A. or B.S. programs.

Articulation to and from the Applied Associate Degree: Challenges and Opportunities

Jan M. Ignash

In September 2010, the Lumina Foundation for Education convened a group of 115 experts in higher education and workforce development, many of them from state educational agencies throughout the United States, to discuss "Applied Baccalaureate Developments and Future Implications." As the two-day session progressed, it was clear that some participants had embraced the applied baccalaureate degree as one of the ways in which to increase educational attainment levels in their states. Participants from other states, however, expressed concerns about the degree—its transferability, its credibility, its feasibility.

This discussion isn't new. It could be argued that the difference of opinion is based on perceptions about education that go back to the Greeks and the Romans, when the so-called "manual arts" were separate—and less exalted—than the academic arts. As community colleges developed in the United States, occupational/technical degrees were often considered lesser degrees than transfer academic degrees because they were *terminal*, a term that, it has been argued, should have been laid to rest years ago (Cohen and Ignash, 1993). Students have been transferring quite successfully from applied associate to baccalaureate programs and, from there into graduate programs, for decades.

Beyond the perceived status differences among the types of degrees students can earn—a topic that has been well-discussed elsewhere—are

NEW DIRECTIONS FOR COMMUNITY COLLEGES, no. 158, Summer 2012 © 2012 Wiley Periodicals, Inc.
Published online in Wiley Online Library (wileyonlinelibrary.com) • DOI: 10.1002/cc.20013

pragmatic issues about the sheer complexity of successfully articulating these degrees. Townsend and Barnes (2001) wrote that tying transfer to the type of associate degree a student earned created "a tangled knot that should be untangled" (p. 132). In another earlier study of two-year college students in Wisconsin, Findlen (1997–1998) found that students in technical programs wanted to transfer, that technical college courses did indeed transfer, and that transferring technical students outnumbered transfer students in other types of programs. So why is the transfer of students in occupational and technical programs, and the articulation of the credits in these programs, still an issue?

The answer may lie, at least in part, because articulating applied associate (A.A.S.) degrees (or non-liberal arts degrees, or occupational/technical degrees, or whatever "nonacademic" appellation is used) tests our views of the curriculum. It blurs the lines between what we consider *applied* versus *academic*, what *general education* is, and how we structure knowledge. Other issues also complicate articulation from A.A.S.-to-baccalaureate degrees, such as the sometimes multiple accrediting and licensing bodies that must be satisfied. An additional hurdle is the fact that articulating an A.A.S. degree to a baccalaureate program is often considered "after the fact," that is, after the program has operated for a period of time and has proven successful. But fundamentally, the question is still often one of the status of the degree, whether or not that is directly acknowledged, and not about curriculum.

This chapter focuses predominantly on curricular hurdles in articulating A.A.S.-to-baccalaureate degrees, because curriculum is generally thought to be the major stumbling block. A model describing three pathways for A.A.S. transfer, developed some years ago by this author, will be used as a lens with which to view examples of existing programs that illustrate the pathways. The author also compares the three A.A.S.-to-baccalaureate pathways in the model to similar B.A. or B.S. programs that are not specifically designed for A.A.S. students in order to highlight the extent of curricular differences that may—or may not—be present. The chapter concludes with an observation that curriculum is less of a stumbling block than we think it is. The "why" and the "who" in A.A.S. to baccalaureate transfer are more important concerns. We need to develop A.A.S. degrees that transfer successfully for both individual and public benefit—because students need these opportunities, and because states need to increase educational attainment.

The Purposes of the Applied Associate Degree: Different Pathways to the Baccalaureate

Applied associate degrees serve different purposes for students and employers. Some degrees build upon one or more underlying certificate programs.

Others have clear employment options. Still others prepare students more broadly for a number of different jobs or careers.

In a national survey of occupational transfer conducted almost fifteen years ago, this author found that twenty-two states reported providing some direction to institutions on standards for the A.A.S. degree, standards that tended to address general education and credit hour minimums but not much else (Ignash, 1997). At that time, a statement expressed by one state official was indicative of the regard with which the A.A.S. degree was commonly held: "Articulation from our technical associate degree programs into baccalaureate programs has improved in recent years. . . . However, in most places these degrees are still not equal to the transfer degrees" (Ignash, 1997, p. 8).

When the author and another researcher repeated and expanded the study seven years later, considerable progress had been made in addressing the transferability of applied associate degrees (Ignash and Kotun, 2005). Not only did the researchers find that more A.A.S. degrees transferred, but also that different pathways in transferring A.A.S. degrees had developed. Thirty-one of forty responding states had articulation agreements to transfer an occupational/technical associate degree to an applied baccalaureate (B.A.S.) degree in specific fields (Ignash and Kotun, 2005), called a *career ladder* pathway. Far and away the most common was nursing, followed by computer science and engineering fields (Ignash and Kotun, 2005). Ten states reported developing *upside down* or *inverted* baccalaureate degrees, in which general education coursework that students typically take during freshman and sophomore years is taken later, during junior and senior years, and technical coursework is taken during the first two years at the community college. A third type of A.A.S. degree transfer pathway, called a *management ladder* or *capstone* degree, was developed in eight states. In this type of pathway, a B.A.S. degree "tops off" a two-year occupational/technical degree with additional general education courses as well as broad-based courses within the field (Ignash and Kotun, 2005, pp. 115–116).

The major difference between the upside down degree and the management ladder or capstone degree is the focus upon a definite career track. In an upside down degree, students in two-year occupational/technical programs typically graduate with a bachelor of arts degree, a liberal arts degree that does not indicate a specific career objective, although the technical coursework taken during the first two years tells employers about job-specific knowledge and skills a graduate possesses. In a management ladder or capstone degree, graduates are typically awarded a bachelor's of applied science (B.A.S.) or a bachelor's of applied technology (B.A.T.). For many graduates of management ladder or capstone degrees, their career goal is expanded supervisory or management positions, affording them more options within a broader occupational cluster as well as options for graduate study within the field.

Blurring the Lines: What Is Applied Learning . . . and What Is Not?

The way in which the traditional U.S. undergraduate curriculum is divided into lower-division general education and upper-division major coursework merits scrutiny. Is general education really "general" when students can choose from hundreds of humanities or social science courses to fulfill general requirements? How much general education is "pure?" How much of it is applied?

It is important to ask ourselves these questions because occupational/technical programs have always been understood to be applied and therefore different from purely academic programs. In her excellent work *Learning to Think*, Janet Donald (2002) discusses the difference between pure and applied:

> Pure disciplines are more likely to use specific models, whereas applied areas are more open to environmental complexity and eclecticism—using the most fitting model or method in a given circumstance. For example, in physics scientists test theories; in contrast in engineering the criterion of success is what works . . . Applied areas of study are sometimes described as fields because the phenomenon they study are relatively unrestricted and the methods, frequently taken from several disciplines, are diverse. Education, for example, is considered to be a field because it incorporates knowledge and methods from a variety of disciplines, both in traditional subject matter areas such as history or English, and in the social sciences (p. 10).

Given Donald's definitions above, shouldn't engineering and education (both applied fields) award bachelor in applied science (B.A.S.) degrees—rather than bachelor of arts (B.A.) or bachelor of science (B.S.) degrees to four-year graduates? What about business? Can there be such a degree as a B.A.S. in applied management? And if there is, how would it differ from a B.S. in management—in curriculum, in job and career options, and in graduate school options?

Using an example from each of the three types of A.A.S. to baccalaureate degree pathways (management ladder or capstone, career ladder, and upside down degree) developed by Ignash and Kotun (2005), we will examine the target student audience and the curricular structure of each of the three pathways and compare them to similar "regular" B.A. or B.S. programs.

Example of a Management Ladder or Capstone Pathway.   Business is a field in which we increasingly find both B.A. or B.S. degrees as well as B.A.S. degrees and provides a ready example of a management ladder or capstone pathway. Donald's definition (above) of a curriculum that deals more with environmental complexity and eclecticism than in testing "pure" theories can apply to undergraduate business degrees.

NEW DIRECTIONS FOR COMMUNITY COLLEGES • DOI: 10.1002/cc

The B.A.S. in applied management at Columbia Basin College, a predominantly two-year college, is a management ladder or capstone pathway because students who have earned a minimum of ninety quarter credit hours in an applied associate degree in *any* field can apply to the program. Marketing materials for the college's B.A.S. in applied management clearly defines the target audience and the purpose for the A.A.S.-to-B.A.S. pathway of these degrees, welcoming students with A.A.S. degrees in automotive, health care, small business, and other majors:

> This degree is designed for those who have earned an Associate of Applied Science (AAS) degree, but lack the broader business-related education needed to move into leadership positions. Many AAS holders have reached a plateau in their career, unable to advance because they cannot meet the bachelor's degree requirements for many supervisory positions. The BAS degree will broaden career opportunities and help graduates climb the career ladder leading to improved chances for promotion to management positions. The BAS program is designed specifically for AAS graduates because their applied science credits are generally non-transferable to four-year institutions. The program gives AAS holders an opportunity to pursue a bachelor's degree without having to start their college education from scratch . . . (Columbia Basin College, 2010).

The curriculum totals a minimum of 180 quarter credit hours (120 semester hours) and sprinkles fifty-five quarter credit hours of general education throughout the upper-division coursework. Table 2.1 shows the structure of the B.A.S. degree in applied management at Columbia Basin College and compares it to a BA in business administration at the state's

Table 2.1.   Comparison of B.A. in Business Administration and B.A.S. in Applied Management

Overall Structure of the Degree	Credits in B.A.[1]	Credits in B.A.S.[2]
Total Credits to Degree (quarter hour)	180 minimum	180 minimum
General Education Requirements	59	55
Business Courses	72	55
1) Lower-Division Business Core	(19)	(45)
2) Upper-Division Business Core	(37)	(10)
3) Upper-Division Business Electives	(16)	70
Workforce Foundation: Transfer from A.A.S.		
Electives and Other Requirements	To equal 180 minimum	5 to 10

[1] University of Washington, Foster School of Business, Bachelor of Arts (B.A.) in Business Administration, 2001.
[2] Columbia Basin College, Bachelor of Applied Science (B.A.S.) in Applied Management, 2010.

flagship institution. Both programs are approved in the state and by the Northwest Regional Accrediting Association.

If we compare the program requirements for the B.A.S. in applied management at Columbia Basin College to the B.A. in business administration at the University of Washington, we see that the general education component does not differ significantly. A closer look at the content of the B.A.S. in applied management at Columbia Basin College also reveals that the upper-division general education courses integrate general studies content within the applied management field. Below are two course descriptions from the program that illustrate this point:

ENVS 310 Environmental Issues

Basic concepts of ecology and environmental science are discussed and illustrated through lab experiences and then further elaborated through discussing environmental issues from a strategic business perspective. Discussions include how environmental pressures (e.g. sustainable development) and environmental problems (e.g. global warming, air pollution, waste-disposal), impact corporate mission, competitive strategy, technology choices, product development decisions, production processes, and corporate responsibility.

ICS 310 American Diversity

This course begins by defining diversity and then proceeds to examine the Workforce 2000 study and subsequent data from the U.S. Census Bureau showing how the demographics of the United States workforce and the economy at large are changing. This class provides a short history, cultural overview, and perspective about contemporary American diversity. Special attention is paid to Native Americans, Hispanic Americans, Asian Americans, and African Americans. Important topics include labor relations, race relations, and historic and modern patterns of migration and immigration. Each student develops a plan as to how a business/company should prepare for and respond to the changing workforce (Columbia Basin College, 2010).

Some differences do exist for courses and credits in the major, although the same topics appear to be covered in both programs. The University of Washington lists statistics as a lower-division business requirement. Columbia Basin lists statistics as a math requirement. Columbia Basin requires students in the program to take forty-five credits in upper-division business courses, about two or three courses more than the University of Washington requires, most likely to allow room in the curriculum to cover content that University of Washington students took in their freshman and sophomore years. For example, managerial accounting and financial accounting are two separate five-credit lower-division courses for University of Washington students; for students at Columbia Basin College, financial and managerial accounting is a five-credit course taken at the upper-division level.

NEW DIRECTIONS FOR COMMUNITY COLLEGES • DOI: 10.1002/cc

Example of a Career Ladder Pathway.   The second of the three A.A.S.-to-baccalaureate pathways we will examine is the *career ladder* pathway. The A.A.S. degree career ladder pathway, as often developed in nursing or other health fields, is usually a fairly straightforward pathway regarding the purpose and the target student population.

An example from Bellevue College shows the career ladder pathway in the field of interior design. The college designed the program to encourage students in A.A.S. in interior design programs at other two-year colleges to transfer into a bachelor of applied arts (B.A.A.) program, thus providing a pathway for better employment prospects and possibilities for advancement (Washington Higher Education Coordinating Board [HECB], 2009). The profession is regulated by the Council for Interior Design Accreditation, which raised the bar for certified interior design professionals to a minimum of a bachelor's degree in 2010. Bellevue College's B.A.A. in interior design was developed, therefore, in response to changes in accreditation. The college's former A.A.S. degree program, which was almost three years in length, was redesigned to address changes in training levels for graduates in the field. The new curriculum follows a 2+2 design, with ninety-seven credits in an A.A.S. program that aligns with the B.A.A. in interior design, the only degree of its kind in the state.

The college's marketing materials for this degree clearly note that enrollment is restricted to those students who have earned an applied degree within the field, stating that the B.A.A. program is an upper-division course of study for students "who have completed a two year foundation in interior design-related studies" (Bellevue College, Bachelor of Applied Arts in Interior Design, n.d.).

Table 2.2 compares the general structure of the B.A.A. in interior design at Bellevue College to a bachelor of arts (B.A.) degree program

Table 2.2.   **Comparison of B.A. and B.A.A. in Interior Design: General Structure of the Degree**

Structure of the Degree	BA[1] *(converted to quarter hours)*	BAA[2]
Total Credits	120 (semester) = 180 quarter	191 quarter
General Education	40 (semester); 60 quarter	75 quarter (with some courses overlapping with core interior design requirements)
Interior Design Courses	80 (semester); 120 quarter	133 quarter (some overlap with general education requirements)
		(72 quarter from A.A.S. degree)
		(61 upper division)

[1] Washington State University, Department of Interior Design, Bachelor of Arts (B.A.) Degree, 2011.
[2] Bellevue College, Bachelor of Applied Arts (B.A.A.) Degree, 2010.

offered by one of the state's research universities. Major requirements for the two programs are not all that different, but the programs do vary somewhat in the amount of design studio work. While at the institute, students in the university program take four courses labeled Design Studio (IV through VII), which focus on individual and team projects. At Bellevue College's B.A.A. in interior design, students also must complete two design studio capstone courses as well as a variety of interior design projects as part of each course's requirements. The coursework does appear to be more structured, however, with specific topics more likely to be spelled out. Nevertheless, both programs—the B.A. at the four-year university and the B.A.S. at Bellevue College—have strong applied components.

Interestingly, the program at the research university could also be said to follow a 2+2 model, because students at the upper-division level are required to move to another campus in another city to attend an interdisciplinary design institute.

Example of the Upside-Down Degree Pathway: Evergreen State College.   Evergreen State College was one of the first in the United States to establish an *"upside-down"* degree, the third A.A.S.-to-baccalaureate degree pathway discussed in this chapter. Following this pathway, students who have a two-year technical degree in an approved field can pursue a bachelor of arts (B.A.) degree by taking ninety credits in liberal arts, with a minimum of thirty-two credits in coordinated studies outside the academic area of the two-year degree upon transfer to Evergreen (The Evergreen State College, 2011). A student applies to Evergreen for the upside-down degree and, if accepted, a maximum of ninety quarter credit hours are held "in escrow" until the student successfully completes ninety credit hours of liberal studies at the College.

The upside-down degree is not unlike a bachelor's in general studies, which many universities offer, with one exception—the target student audience. The upside-down degree provides a baccalaureate pathway for students who have completed an approved technical associate degree (A.A.S. or Associate in Applied Technology [A.A.T.]) while the B.A. in general studies degree targets students who have completed an academic transfer degree (A.A.).

An example from Western Washington University provides an opportunity to compare the upside-down degree A.A.S.-to-baccalaureate pathway with a "regular" transfer degree pathway, that of an associate of arts (A.A.)-to-B.A. pathway. The B.A. in general studies degree from Western Washington University is designed to provide

> . . . a solid liberal arts education to prepare students for rapidly changing career opportunities in many different fields. It is designed for students whose interests cannot be served by Western's established majors, and who want to focus their major studies across courses and departments to better meet their career goals or preparation for advanced levels of education (Western Washington University, College of Humanities and Social Sciences, 2010).

Table 2.3.   Comparing the Upside-Down Degree and B.A. in General Studies Degree Pathways

Structure of the Degree	BA in General Studies[1]	Upside-Down Degree[2]
Total Credits	180 (quarter hours)	180
Lower Division	60 credits	Up to 90 credits
	(A.A. two-year transfer degree program or university General Undergraduate Requirements)	(any A.A.S. or A.A.T. two-year degree program)
Upper Division	60 credits	90 credits in liberal studies
Thematic Areas:	(35 credits)	(32 credits in coordinated
• Social Sciences		studies outside the area of
• Sciences		the two-year degree)
• Humanities		
• Business		
• Health		
• Liberal Arts		
Elective Credits	(25 credits)	
• Any Area, including Thematic Area		
• 300–400 level		

[1] Western Washington University, College of Humanities and Social Sciences, 2010.
[2] The Evergreen State College, 2011.

Table 2.3 compares the general structure of the two degrees—the upside-down A.A.S.-to-B.A. pathway and an A.A. to B.A. in general studies at a four-year university in the same state. As with the other two A.A.S.-to-baccalaureate pathways discussed in this chapter, the overall structure of the two degrees is similar.

Curriculum, Purpose, Target Student Audience: A.A.S.-to-Baccalaureate Pathways

The preceding review of A.A.S. degree pathways to a baccalaureate degree—whether B.A.S., B.A.A., or B.A.—shows how loose our curricular definitions of *applied* versus pure can be. From the examples in this chapter, it appears that the lines are too blurred to insist that a B.A.S. degree program in, say, applied management is significantly "less pure" or "more applied" than a B.A. in business administration. So how much of a hurdle does the applied nature of curriculum cause in transfer?

When this author first undertook a study of A.A.S. degree transfer fifteen years ago in 1997, respondents reported that transferring the general education component of technical degrees was a real hurdle. General education courses in English and math were often developed to respond to the demands of the field for technical writing or math—and they were not developed with an eye toward transferability. Only one state, Maryland, required transferable general education coursework in the A.A.S. degree. By 2005, however, twenty-three of forty states required transferable general education to be part of occupational/technical degrees.

Today, as more transfer agreements have been developed for more A.A.S. degree programs, we have gotten better at ensuring that the general education portion of A.A.S. programs does indeed transfer. Curriculum developers more frequently consider the transferability of A.A.S. degree courses and programs, including the general education component, as part of the work they do in developing new programs. We have more examples to draw from as transfer from A.A.S. to baccalaureate programs has expanded. Columbia Basin College's B.A.S. in applied management is a good example of how curriculum developers are integrating upper-division general education content into the program major.

So if the curriculum is less of a stumbling block in developing A.A.S.-to-baccalaureate pathways, why do we still struggle with encouraging more students in A.A.S. degree programs to complete baccalaureate degrees? Are we artificially creating differences?

The more important concerns, even over curriculum, in successfully articulating A.A.S. degree holders to baccalaureates today concern "why" and "who," rather than "what."

The art of successfully articulating A.A.S. degrees lies in being crystal clear about intent and target audience—why students and employers believe additional education beyond the A.A.S. degree is important. Do supervisory or management options exist within the career for which a bachelor's degree is expected? Or do most supervisors or managers attain those positions because of personal qualities or demonstrated expertise within the field? Would completion of a bachelor's degree provide any career, promotion, or salary advantage? Is a graduate degree becoming more and more common for upper levels of the pay scale in a field? Would a bachelor's degree provide broader career options and better job prospects?

Arguably, the biggest concern of all in developing more A.A.S.-to-baccalaureate degree pathways is about the "who," the students. The marketing materials from several of the colleges cited in this chapter clearly identify the target students. The language approving new programs by Washington state's higher education agencies also clearly identifies the target student audience:

> [The purpose of the BAS degree is to] [i]ncrease educational pathways for professional and technical associate graduates who have been limited in their ability to apply credits toward a bachelor degree. The workforce student pop-

ulation is comprised of a large portion of people of color, older working adults, and people (women) who are place bound with family responsibilities (Washington State Board for Community and Technical Colleges, 2006).

And again,

> A new way in which Washington can increase baccalaureate degree production is through awarding a relatively new type of degree—the applied baccalaureate degree (B.A.S.). These are degrees specifically designed for individuals who hold an associate of applied science (A.A.S.) degree, or its equivalent, in order to maximize application of their technical course credits toward the baccalaureate degree (Washington Higher Education Coordinating Board, 2010).

Conclusions and Implications

Although sticking points remain regarding the articulation of A.A.S.-to-baccalaureate degrees, just as they do in articulating almost *any* degree, it seems higher education has made progress in untangling the knot of transferring applied associate degrees. Over the past several decades, we have made significant progress in designing more A.A.S. programs that transfer successfully to baccalaureate programs and can no longer blame the curriculum as an insurmountable barrier. We have found more ways to integrate general education throughout upper-division coursework. And we have obviously communicated our expectations to students in A.A.S. programs that transfer is possible, because more of them are indeed transferring.

This chapter began by noting that our perceptions of the value of education arguably goes back to the Greeks and the Romans, when status awarded to the academic arts was greater than that awarded to the more lowly "manual arts." It is perhaps fitting, then, to end this chapter with another reference to the ancient world, that of Janus, the god of beginnings and transitions, as borrowed from Clark (1987) who observed that education has both intellectual and practical missions and described this dilemma as facing, Janus-like, in two directions. The complexity of articulating applied programs throughout the seams of undergraduate and graduate education can be a complex task. It does not, however, relieve educators from the job of figuring it out.

References

Bellevue College, Bachelor of Applied Arts in Interior Design, n.d., at http://bellevuecollege.edu/programs/degrees/bachelor/baa

Bellevue College: Interior Studies. Associate in Arts Degree. 2010–2011 Requirements, 2010, at http://bellevuecollege.edu/worksheets/pdfs/AA/Interior_Studies.pdf

Clark, B. B. R. *The Academic Life: Small Worlds, Different Worlds*. Princeton, N.J.: Carnegie Foundation for the Advancement of Teaching, 1987.

New Directions for Community Colleges • DOI: 10.1002/cc

Cohen. A. M., and Ignash, J. M. "The Scope and Transferability of Occupational Courses in the Two-Year College." *Community College Review*, 1993, *21*(3), 68–76.

Columbia Basin College. Bachelor of Applied Science in Management. Program Handbook 2010–2011. Pasco, WA: Author, 2010.

Donald, J. G. "Learning to Think: Disciplinary Perspectives." San Francisco: Jossey-Bass, 2002.

Evergreen State College. "Admissions. The Upside Down Degree Program." Admissions, Evergreen State College Web site, 2011, at http://admissions.evergreen.edu/upsidedown.html

Findlen, G. L. "Technical Colleges and College Transfer—One More Time." *ATEA Journal*, Dec 1997–Jan 1998, *25*(2), 4–7. (EJ 556 443.)

Ignash, J. M. *Results of an Investigation of State Policies for the AAS Degree.* Springfield, Ill.: Illinois Board of Higher Education, 1997. (ED 405 051.)

Ignash, J. M., and Kotun, D. "Results of a National Study of Transfer in Occupational/Technical Degrees: Policies and Practices." *Journal of Applied Research in the Community College*, Spring 2005, *12*(2), 109–120.

Townsend, B. K., and Barnes, T. "Tying Transfer to Type of Associate Degree: A Tangled Knot." *Journal of Applied Research in the Community College*, Spring 2001, *8*(2), 125–133.

University of Washington: Foster School of Business. The Bachelor of Arts in Business Administration Degree. UW Foster School of Business Web site, 2001, at www.foster.washington.edu/academic/undergrad/Pages/BABADegree.aspx

Washington Higher Education Coordinating Board (HECB). "Bachelor of Applied Arts in Interior Design." (2009, July 28).

Washington Higher Education Coordinating Board (HECB). "Proposed Applied Baccalaureate Selection Process and Criteria" (board item), HECB Meeting Agenda, November 2010.

Washington State Board for Community and Technical Colleges (SBCTC). "Applied Baccalaureate Degrees at Community and Technical Colleges." Olympia, WA.: State Board for Community and Technical Colleges (2006).

Washington State University. Department of Interior Design. Core Courses. Washington State University Web Site, 2011, at http://id.wsu.edu/undergraduate/core-courses

Western Washington University. College of Humanities and Social Sciences. "2010 Catalog." Bellingham, WA.: Western Washington University (2010).

JAN M. IGNASH is the vice chancellor and chief academic officer of the Florida Board of Governors for the State University System. Previously, she was the Deputy Director of Policy, Planning and Research for the Washington Higher Education Coordinating Board.

3

This chapter shares how the state of Washington embraces the use of applied baccalaureate degrees at community colleges as a way to help meet employer demands and statewide degree production goals.

Washington State's Model and Programs: Applied Baccalaureate Degrees at Community and Technical Colleges

Christy England-Siegerdt, Michelle Andreas

President Obama is calling for an increase in educational attainment among citizens of the United States (Obama, 2009). Prior to this national call, Washington State recognized the need to increase the educational attainment of its residents to maintain a globally competitive economy. By 2018, 67 percent of jobs in Washington will require a postsecondary education (Carnevale, Smith, and Strohl, 2010). Historically, Washington businesses relied heavily on the ability to import educated workers. However, this practice may not be sustainable or sufficient enough to meet the changing needs of the workforce (Spaulding, 2010). Yet limited state resources prevent public baccalaureate institutions from developing the capacity needed to meet current and projected employer demand and statewide degree production goals.

Washington's Higher Education and Coordinating Board (HECB) and State Board for Community and Technical Colleges (SBCTC) identified applied baccalaureate degrees as a viable option for substantially increasing the number of baccalaureate degrees awarded over the next twenty years. Applied baccalaureate degrees will help the state achieve degree production goals by creating opportunities for professional and technical associate degree graduates who are traditionally unable to transfer credits toward a baccalaureate degree program. An applied baccalaureate degree is also an

New Directions for Community Colleges, no. 158, Summer 2012 © 2012 Wiley Periodicals, Inc.
Published online in Wiley Online Library (wileyonlinelibrary.com) • DOI: 10.1002/cc.20014

innovative and attractive strategy for adult learners seeking to upgrade their skills or to earn a promotion (Bragg, Townsend, & Ruud, 2009).

The Need for Applied Baccalaureate Degrees in Washington

In spring 2002, the SBCTC began exploring the potential for community and technical colleges to offer and award applied baccalaureate degrees as part of a discussion surrounding baccalaureate degree access for community and technical college students, particularly for technical degree graduates (SBCTC, January 2002). One of the challenges facing the higher education system at the time was upper-division capacity (SBCTC, May 2004). Capacity was and still is an issue for the public baccalaureate institutions in particular. Projections showed that public baccalaureate institutions would be unable to increase enrollments and expand program offerings at rates that would keep pace with population growth and student demand. In addition, there were geographic regions where place bound students did not have easy access to baccalaureate programs, especially in high-demand professional and technical fields (SBCTC, May 2004).

Later studies revealed that employers in fields such as health and social services were raising the education and credential requirements for jobs previously held by associate degree holders (SBCTC, January 2005). In addition, employers were seeking a way to increase the education of current technically proficient employees so that they could promote them into management positions. Though employers in Washington supported the need for more options, Washington's four-year institutions provided very few options for technical degree holders (SBCTC, May 2004, May 2005). Most of the existing opportunities were available through private institutions and most were located in the western region of the state. The options available through public baccalaureate institutions included four applied programs (i.e., information technology, safety and health management, industrial technology, and food service management) offered by Central Washington University, an applied technology option in the bachelor of science degree offered by Eastern Washington University, and an upside down degree option offered by The Evergreen State College.

The Legislature Responds

In the spring of 2005, the Washington legislature expanded access to baccalaureate degree programs through the passage of House Bill 1794. The bill included several provisions aimed at increasing access to baccalaureate degree programs, including a pilot project at community and technical colleges that allowed the SBCTC to select four colleges to offer a baccalaureate degree program in an applied field. The bill also recognized the Higher Education Coordinating Board's (HECB) authority to approve all baccalaureate- and graduate-level programs in the state. As a result, the new applied baccalaureate programs at the community and technical colleges required approval from both the SBCTC and the HECB.

The legislation also included the following definition of an applied baccalaureate program:

> An applied baccalaureate degree is specifically designed for individuals who hold an associate of applied science degree, or its equivalent, in order to maximize application of their technical course credits toward the baccalaureate degree; and it is based on a curriculum that incorporates both theoretical and applied knowledge and skills in a specific technical field (RCW 28B.50.030, 2009).

The legislation also specified that the programs were to serve place bound working adults and fill skill gap needs in specific high-demand occupations.

In 2005, the legislature provided $100,000 to help pilot colleges begin developing programs and provided $6,300 per FTE to support forty full-time equivalent students in each program. In 2008, the legislature authorized the SBCTC to select three additional colleges to participate in the pilot program with the same funding arrangement as the initial pilot programs.

Approving the Pilot Programs

The definition outlined in statute was central to the development of the selection criteria and process used to identify and authorize colleges to offer applied baccalaureate degrees. A task force comprised of community and technical college representatives and staff from the SBCTC, the HECB, the Workforce Training and Education Coordinating Board (WTECB), and the Northwest Commission on Colleges and Universities (NWCCU) was charged with developing the selection criteria (SBCTC, 2005). The task force started by establishing the following principals to guide the development of the criteria.

- The program must serve students from the area not otherwise served by existing public baccalaureate degree programs.
- The program must be an extension of the college's workforce mission and respond to increasing skill requirements of employers in occupations traditionally served by community and technical colleges.
- Pilot colleges must have the capacity to develop and sustain new programs and have a history of good use of resources.
- Colleges must remain predominantly lower-division institutions.
- Colleges must maintain the open-door mission common to all CTCs in Washington.

The initial selection process required colleges to submit an application to SBCTC by January 2006 (SBCTC, 2005). Six colleges submitted applications. SBCTC convened an evaluation committee with representation from community college presidents, instruction, student services, and business administration; SBCTC staff; universities offering applied bachelor's degrees; and a workforce representative (SBCTC, 2006). The committee identified four colleges with the strongest proposals and recommended that they be selected for the pilot program: Bellevue Community College, Olympic College, Peninsula College, and South Seattle Community College. These four colleges applied for and received approval from the HECB in July 2006. Once approved, pilot colleges began program development and made application to the NWCCU for accreditation approval as baccalaureate granting institutions. A similar process followed after the 2008 legislature authorized the selection of three additional pilot programs.

Between July 2006 and July 2009, the following eight applied baccalaureate degree programs at seven colleges were approved as pilot programs.

- Bachelor of applied science (B.A.S.) in radiation and imaging sciences at Bellevue College (approved July 26, 2006)
- B.A.S. in applied management at Peninsula College (approved July 26, 2006)
- Bachelor of science in nursing at Olympic College (approved July 27, 2006)
- B.A.S. in hospitality management at South Seattle Community College (approved July 26, 2006)
- B.A.S. in applied management at Columbia Basin College (approved July 22, 2008)
- Bachelor of technology in applied design at Lake Washington Technical College (approved July 22, 2008)
- B.A.S. in applied behavioral sciences at Seattle Central Community College (approved July 22, 2008)
- Bachelor of applied arts in interior design at Bellevue College (approved July 28, 2009)

The first four programs began enrolling students in fall 2007. A total of ninety full-time equivalent (FTE) students enrolled during the 2007–2008 academic year, growing to 143 FTEs in 2008–2009. By 2009–2010, with all of the above programs in place, enrollment grew to 246 FTEs. A total of thirty-five degrees were awarded to students in the first four programs by the end of the 2008–2009 academic year, and an additional fifty-seven degrees were awarded during 2009–2010.

Making the Case for Additional Degree Programs

More recent analyses completed during the development of the HECB *2008 Strategic Master Plan for Higher Education in Washington* (HECB, 2007) and the SBCTC's *Mission Study* (SBCTC, 2010) showed a quickening dilemma regarding increased baccalaureate capacity and production: The state's share of resources allocated to higher education has been decreasing while its population has been growing, especially among populations that are underrepresented in the educational system—students from low-income families, first-generation students, and people of color. The *Strategic Master Plan* estimates that statewide bachelor's degree production needs to increase by 13,800 annually. Clearly, the public baccalaureate institutions cannot assume the full weight, since they do not have the capacity to meet projected demand. The public baccalaureate institutions also do not have the capacity to accept the estimated 20,400 annual transfer students seeking baccalaureate degrees, let alone the professional and technical associate degree graduates seeking a bachelor's degree (SBCTC, 2010).

As a follow-up to the strategic master plan, the HECB developed *The System Design Plan* (2009). The plan was intended to provide a framework for making decisions in a way that would support the goals of the strategic master plan. The strategies for increasing baccalaureate degree production included a recommendation to expand the availability of applied baccalaureate degrees at community and technical colleges, as did SBCTC's 2010 *Mission Study*.

Again the legislature responded favorably to the call for increased capacity. In spring 2010, the legislature endorsed the recommendations for increasing baccalaureate degree production outlined in HECB's system design plan through Senate Substitute Bill 6355. This bill removed the pilot status from applied baccalaureate degrees at community and technical colleges and removed the limitation on the number of colleges that could offer these programs.

The Current Approval Process and Criteria

Staff from the SBCTC and the HECB spent the remainder of 2010 developing a joint approval process and application for applied baccalaureate degree programs at the community and technical colleges (HECB, 2010; SBCTC, 2010). Staff from both agencies agreed upon two key goals for the new process. First, the process needed to allow both boards to retain their individual approval authority over applied baccalaureate programs. This goal was met by incorporating specific points in the process for each board to approve an application as described below. Second, staff wanted to minimize the paperwork for the institutions by developing a single application and review process.

In the new process, both boards retain their individual approval authority while using one set of approval criteria, a single application, and one approval process. Merging board-approved criteria was also critical to developing a single application and approval process. The new approval process includes five steps.

1. *Intent.* Colleges must notify the SBCTC, the HECB, and other higher education institutions of their intent to offer an applied baccalaureate degree program. Colleges simply submit the working title of the program and the anticipated enrollment date for new students.
2. *Statement of Need.* Colleges submit the Statement of Need Application to SBCTC. SBCTC board members and staff will invite staff from the college to engage in a study session. The focus of the session will be the relationship of the program to the mission, vision, and goals of the college and the overall community and technical college system. If the program aligns with the college and system goals, staff from the SBCTC and HECB will conduct a joint review of the statement of need to determine whether there is sufficient demand for the program. If so, all higher education institutions in Washington will have 30 days to submit comments and feedback regarding the proposed program. This comment period provides an opportunity for other institutions to notify the SBCTC and HECB of other plans or initiatives that may already be under way, thereby providing the SBCTC and HECB with an opportunity to discuss and determine the best route for meeting specific workforce needs in a given region.
3. *Approval Application and Review.* Following approval of the Statement of Need Application, institutions have twelve months to submit a full program approval application. Staff from the SBCTC and HECB will convene a committee of higher education representatives to review the application. The review committee will include community and technical college vice presidents of instruction, student services, and finance/business; a community or technical college president; representatives from a university and the Workforce Training and Education Board; and others as appropriate. The committee will make recommendations to the SBCTC.
4. *SBCTC Approval.* The SBCTC will review the recommendation from the review committee and decide whether to approve the program.
5. *HECB Approval.* If the SBCTC approves the program, the HECB Education Committee will review the application and determine whether the program should be submitted to the entire board for approval. If the program is endorsed by the Education Committee and staff, the program will be submitted for consideration.

Lessons Learned Thus Far

Colleges and policymakers have learned a great deal about implementing applied baccalaureate degree programs in community and technical colleges. Following is a description of critical issues for policymakers to consider. Several key lessons learned by staff from the seven pilot institutions during a recent discussion about the process of developing and implementing applied baccalaureate institutions are also summarized in this section.

NEW DIRECTIONS FOR COMMUNITY COLLEGES • DOI: 10.1002/cc

For Policymakers. Particularly during recessions, policymakers need to work closely with colleges to identify statewide baccalaureate needs. Since the Washington legislature authorized the development of pilot programs, the state experienced drastic reductions in state revenue and reduced funding for public higher education. Though the legislature provided a modest amount of seed money to support the pilot programs, institutions relied largely upon the reduced state appropriations or other fund sources in order to implement the applied baccalaureate degree programs. As Washington continues to face additional reductions to state revenue and funding for higher education, it is imperative for Washington's citizens and economy to continue finding ways to implement these programs. By thoroughly analyzing workforce needs and student demand, the state and the colleges can better target their resources toward programs that will be of the most value to employers, students, and the state.

Policymakers also need to provide an efficient application and review process so that colleges can be responsive to community needs. As previously noted, primary authority for baccalaureate and graduate degree programs reside with the HECB, while the SBCTC is responsible for approving degree programs at community and technical colleges. It was a policy priority to develop a single application that would incorporate criteria used by both boards to approve degree programs. The current process requires close coordination and constant communication by staff from both boards in order to process the applications as outlined above.

For Institutions. One of the most beneficial aspects of the applied baccalaureate movement in Washington has been the camaraderie and sharing between and among college faculty and staff as they developed their programs, sought accreditation, admitted their first students, and graduated their first applied baccalaureate candidates. For colleges planning to develop applied baccalaureate programs in the future, the pilot colleges offered the following advice:

• Review the college mission, vision, and values in relation to implementing an applied baccalaureate program. Specific questions debated on campuses included: Would an applied baccalaureate degree program create a mission blur? Would an applied baccalaureate degree program change the direction and focus of the college? What aspect of the mission, vision, and values would be met through an applied baccalaureate degree? Colleges should consider how the program could build on existing program strengths and increase education and career pathways for students.

• Understand the time commitment required for planning and implementing the applied baccalaureate degree. Colleges report that it takes two or three years to get these programs started, and all of the pilot colleges underestimated the time it would take from initiation to implementation.

NEW DIRECTIONS FOR COMMUNITY COLLEGES • DOI: 10.1002/cc

- Get faculty buy-in to the program early in the process. Having faculty involvement early in the program development process helped to acquire overall institutional program support, smooth faculty contract issues, and merge a baccalaureate program into the overall mission of the institution.
- Use local professional and technical program advisory committees comprised of employers to help structure the program, provide curricula content expertise, spread the word about the program, and teach in the program. This helps to ensure students will receive the education and training employers require.
- Pay close attention to the actual costs associated with course development, implementation, and revisions need for a successful program. Specifically, faculty course development costs were greater than anticipated, in part because the courses were new and faculty needed to rework curriculum and assessment content and strategies after initial implementation.
- Acquire sufficient space, equipment, library services, and student support services to serve the new program and its students. The facilities and services needed for upper-division courses and students, depending on the program, may be different from those used for lower-division courses and students. Administrators needed to use baccalaureate curriculum to guide decisions about space, equipment, and services and not assume that current space, equipment, and services were sufficient.
- Recruit students for the program beyond those who may be in the feeder professional and technical program on the campus. Administrators needed to create formal and informal articulation agreements with sister community and technical colleges that offered similar professional and technical associate degree programs to ensure strong and sustainable applied baccalaureate program enrollments.
- Develop articulation agreements for applied baccalaureate graduates to enter graduate degree programs. Members of the HECB and SBCTC, along with other policymakers, expressed interest in ensuring applied baccalaureate degree holders have viable options for continuing their education if they choose to do so.
- Provide ongoing networking opportunities for colleges. Administrators from the seven pilot colleges continue to meet on a quarterly basis to share best practices, resolve potential system barriers for students, and review the needs for future applied baccalaureate programs in the state with policymakers.

Conclusion

Washington, like many other states, must increase the number of citizens that hold a baccalaureate degree in order to compete in a global economy. The HECB and the SBCTC agree that applied baccalaureate degrees are a viable pathway for students who may otherwise struggle or fail to gain access to and graduate with a baccalaureate degree. The pilot programs show great promise, but there is still room for growth in order to meet the state's workforce demands and degree goals.

References

Bragg, D. D., Townsend, B. K., and Ruud, C. M. "The Adult Learner and the Applied Baccalaureate: Emerging Lessons for State and Local Implementation." *In Brief*, 2009, at http://occrl.illinois.edu/files/InBrief/AppBaccBrief.pdf

Carnevale, A. P., Smith, N., and Strohl, J. "Help Wanted: Projections of Jobs and Education Requirements Through 2018." Georgetown University Center on Education and the Workforce Web site, 2010, at http://www9.georgetown.edu/grad/gppi/hpi/cew/pdfs/state-levelanalysis-web.pdf

Obama, B. Remarks of President Barack Obama—As Prepared for Delivery. Address to Joint Session of Congress. White House Web site, 2009, at www.whitehouse.gov/the_press_office/remarks-of-president-barack-obama-Address-to-joint-session-of-congress

RCW 28B.50.030, 2009.

Spaulding, R. S. "The Impact of Interstate Migration on Human Capital Development in Washington." Washington Higher Education Coordinating Board (HECB), 2010.

Washington Higher Education Coordinating Board (HECB). "2008 Strategic Master Plan for Higher Education in Washington." HECB, 2007.

Washington Higher Education Coordinating Board (HECB). "The System Design Plan: A Statewide Plan for Moving the Blue Arrow." HECB, 2009.

Washington Higher Education Coordinating Board (HECB). "Proposed Applied Baccalaureate Selection Process and Criteria." (board item) HECB Meeting Agenda, November 2010.

Washington State Board for Community and Technical Colleges (SBCTC). "Baccalaureate Degree Access for Community and Technical College Students: Policy Discussion." State Board Study Session Agenda Item. SBCTC Meeting Agenda, January 2002, at www.sbctc.ctc.edu/docs/board/agendas/2002/20020116_agenda_jan_sbctc_mtg.pdf

Washington State Board for Community and Technical Colleges (SBCTC). "Progress Report on Transfer Issues." SBCTC Meeting Agenda, May 2004, at www.sbctc.ctc.edu/docs/board/agendas/2004/20040505_agenda_may_sbctc_mtg.pdf

Washington State Board for Community and Technical Colleges (SBCTC). "Baccalaureate Capacity Study Findings and Recommendations." SBCTC Meeting Agenda, January 2005.

Washington State Board for Community and Technical Colleges (SBCTC). "Approval of CTC Bachelor's Degree Selection Criteria and Process." SBCTC Meeting Agenda, May 2005, at www.sbctc.ctc.edu/docs/board/agendas/2005/20051018_agenda_oct_sbctc_mtg.pdf

Washington State Board for Community and Technical Colleges (SBCTC). "Approval of Applied Bachelor's Degree Pilots." SBCTC Meeting Agenda, 2006, at www.sbctc.ctc.edu/docs/board/agendas/2006/20060405_agenda_apr_sbctc_mtg.pdf

Washington State Board for Community and Technical Colleges (SBCTC). *Mission Study: Washington State Community and Technical Colleges.* SBCTC Web site, 2010, at www.sbctc.ctc.edu/docs/sbctc_mission_study-interactive-web.pdf

CHRISTY ENGLAND-SIEGERDT *is the director of research and planning at the Washington Student Achievement Council.*

MICHELLE ANDREAS *is the associate director for education services at the Washington State Board for Community and Technical Colleges.*

4

This chapter highlights the history of workforce baccalaureate degrees in Florida, documents the growth of these programs across the state, and provides a framework for the designation of various degree types and academic requirements. Florida's new College System is described as one of the largest and most innovative systems of higher education for increasing access to four-year workforce baccalaureates.

The Evolution of Workforce Baccalaureate Degrees in Florida

Judith Bilsky, Ian Neuhard, Mary G. Locke

Perspectives on Need and Demand

The State of Florida has been challenged to keep up with the demand for baccalaureate degree production for more than half a century. Fueled first by veterans of World War II and the Korean Conflict, and later by significant and sustained population growth over many decades, Florida's postsecondary infrastructure has struggled to keep pace with the growing number of residents and students seeking college degrees. James Wattenbarger, the architect of Florida's Community College System, wrote prophetically in 1953, "The changing character of the population and the advance of technology make education beyond the twelfth grade necessary . . ." (p. 6). Despite this insight by Florida's higher education leaders, baccalaureate degree attainment for residents over the age of twenty-five still lags behind the majority of the ten most populated states. Of these states, only Texas, Ohio, and Michigan have a lower proportion of residents with bachelor's degrees as noted in Table 4.1.

Another measure of the importance of baccalaureate degree attainment can be found by examining the states with the highest per capita personal income. In the top three states for personal income (Connecticut, New Jersey, and Massachusetts), the average proportion of residents over the age of twenty-five who have attained a bachelor's degree or higher is 36 percent. In Florida, the percentage with a baccalaureate degree is less than 26 percent (U.S. Census Bureau, 2011).

NEW DIRECTIONS FOR COMMUNITY COLLEGES, no. 158, Summer 2012 © 2012 Wiley Periodicals, Inc.
Published online in Wiley Online Library (wileyonlinelibrary.com) • DOI: 10.1002/cc.20015

Table 4.1.   Educational Attainment in the Ten Most Populated States

States Ranked by Population	Population	Percentage with Bachelor's Degree or Higher
California	36,756,666	29.6
Texas	24,326,974	25.3
New York	19,490,297	31.9
Florida	18,328,340	25.8
Illinois	12,901,563	29.9
Pennsylvania	12,488,279	26.3
Ohio	11,485,910	24.1
Michigan	10,003,422	24.7
Georgia	9,685,744	27.5
North Carolina	9,222,414	26.1

Source: U.S. Census Bureau, Resident Population—July 2008 and 2011 Statistical Abstract.

Today, the "knowledge explosion," as well as the pressure of an uncertain economy, is increasing the demand on higher education systems to deliver increased access to relevant, affordable, postsecondary degrees as never before. The astounding pace in the development of new knowledge and information now shapes our daily experience, creating urgent implications for higher education institutions, the emerging workforce, our faculty, and our students that challenge our colleges and universities to redefine their programs, budgets, and priorities.

Since its inception, Florida's Community College System (now the Florida College System or FCS) has helped to provide postsecondary access through the provision of Associate in Arts degrees that are guaranteed to transfer to State University System (SUS) institutions. The State University System expanded from three to eleven institutions during the latter half of the twentieth century, with four of these universities beginning as upper-division-only institutions (Finney, 1997). During these formative years of the SUS, the only option for many students was to receive the first two years of their baccalaureate degrees at a Florida community college and then transfer to a university to complete their junior and senior years.

Now Florida has three of the ten largest public universities in the nation (U.S. Department of Education, 2010), and all eleven SUS institutions offer the full four years of baccalaureate instruction. Applications far exceed available spaces at all of Florida's state universities. During the budget cuts of 2007, many of Florida's universities implemented three-year freshman enrollmant caps which further reduced access to baccalaureate degrees (Tomsho, 2008). Students with strong "B" averages are being turned away from many of Florida's state universities. For the Fall 2011 academic year, the average GPAs for entering freshmen were 3.79 at the University of North Florida, 3.81 at the University of South Florida, 3.82 at the University of Central Florida, 3.90 at Florida State University, and 4.30 at the University of Florida, where weighted GPAs for advanced placement classes have pushed the entry requirement well beyond a perfect "A" average (Travis, 2011).

Growing Concern

For many years, despite an exemplary "2+2" transfer articulation policy between community colleges and state universities, there has been growing concern among legislators and state policymakers regarding insufficient baccalaureate degree production in Florida. While Florida has a history of being one of the top states in the nation for associate degree production, it ranked forty-sixth out of fifty in baccalaureate degree production at the beginning of the last decade. This ranking, combined with the state's transition from an agriculture- and service-based economy into an economy based on technology, healthcare, and other sophisticated industries, made it evident that for the state to reach its economic potential and attract good jobs for its diverse and growing population, it was essential to not only conceptualize but also actualize expanded access to higher education.

Due to the foresight of higher education policymakers and the support of the state legislature, Florida is a long-standing national leader in student transfer policies that optimize movement between and among public and private postsecondary institutions. Section 1007.01, Florida Statutes, describes the intent of the legislature to: "Facilitate articulation and seamless integration of the K20 education system by building and sustaining relationships among K20 public organizations, between public and private organizations, and between the education system as a whole and Florida's communities" (Florida Statutes, §1007.33, 2010).

The purpose of building and sustaining these relationships is to provide for the efficient and effective progression and transfer of students within the education system and to allow students to proceed toward their educational objectives as rapidly as their circumstances permit. It is within this context and for these reasons that Florida has pursued expanding access to the baccalaureate degree, particularly targeting the state's critical need, the technical workforce sectors.

The Evolution of an Idea

In 2001, legislation was developed that authorized community colleges to provide site-determined baccalaureate degrees under certain circumstances. (Florida Statutes, §1007.33, 2002). Additionally, Senate Bill 1162 re-established St. Petersburg Junior College as St. Petersburg College and provided the authority for that institution to grant bachelor of science degrees in nursing and education, and bachelor of applied science (B.A.S.) degrees in technology-related fields (Florida Statutes, §1004.73, 2002). Because the B.A.S. degree was new to Florida, a Bachelor of Applied Science Task Force with representation from both the State University System and the Florida

College System was established in 2005 specifically to "define" bachelor of applied science degree guidelines, with attention to ensuring that the curriculum for B.A.S. degrees in Florida would meet all the expected articulation conventions and requirements of bachelor of arts and bachelor of science degrees awarded in the state.

Mandating stringent academic and technical requirements for this degree was critical to ensuring that students who earned a B.A.S. would not be disadvantaged in the workplace or in pursuing graduate school admissions. During the 2009 legislative session, Section 1007.33 Florida Statutes was amended to include specific requirements for the workforce baccalaureate degree approval process. The statute outlines the criteria a college must include in degree proposals and delineates the timeframes for specified activities. Included in the criteria are an analysis of unmet employment need and a requirement for consultation with other regional colleges and universities. In addition, all Florida colleges must receive Southern Association of Colleges and Schools Level II accreditation status before beginning delivery of any baccalaureate degree program.

The following definition was developed by the B.A.S. Task Force (2006) with special consideration for the issues of academic integrity, articulation, flexibility, workforce preparation, and applied learning:

> The Bachelor of Applied Science (BAS) is the designated degree for flexible baccalaureate programs that are designed to accommodate the unique demands for entry and advancement within specific workforce sectors. BAS programs provide degree completion opportunities for students from a variety of educational backgrounds, but primarily those with A.S. degrees or the equivalent (p. 5).

These thousands of A.S. degree graduates fill a critical role in the provision of essential services; they staff the state's hospitals, law enforcement agencies, technical industries, and growing businesses. They also tend to be somewhat older than traditional college students, employed full-time and place bound by work and family responsibilities. Although Florida employers eagerly hire A.S. graduates, and report consistently high levels of satisfaction with them as employees, advancement opportunities for this population of workers have often been severely hindered by lack of access to baccalaureate degree programs.

Nationally and internationally, B.A.S. degrees have been designed to address specific workforce needs. These needs are diverse and dynamic, encompassing everything from skill development in written communication, oral communication, and critical thinking; to advanced knowledge and technical expertise within specific disciplines; to the need for training in management and administration (Bachelor of Applied Science Task Force, 2006). B.A.S. degree programs conform to all articulation conventions (including common course prerequisites, common course numbering, and faculty credentialing in accordance with the Southern Association of Colleges and Schools). They typically include capstone experiences that provide opportunities for students to demonstrate the applications of acquired knowledge, skills, and competencies. All B.A.S. degrees in Florida require thirty-six hours of General Education and demonstration of foreign language competence. According to the 2006 Bachelor of Applied Science Task Force Final Report, they may be classified into one of four degree structures:

1. *Inverted Baccalaureate*: An upper-division focus on completion of general education requirements, electives, and courses related to the area of concentration.
2. *General Management*: An upper-division focus on general business and management courses.
3. *Advanced Discipline and Management*: An upper-division focus on advanced content in the discipline of the A.S. degree (or equivalent) and management courses.
4. *Discipline Saturation*: An upper-division focus on advanced content in the discipline of the A.S. degree or equivalent.

Each institution in the Florida College System that proposes a baccalaureate degree program works closely with a team of faculty members, administrators, and other professionals from its campus, as well as business and industry advisors, to outline how the program will be implemented and supported. Upon approval from the college's Board of Trustees, each proposal is thoroughly reviewed by a cross-functional team at the Florida Department of Education consisting of staff from the Division of Florida Colleges, the Division of Accountability, Research and Measurement, and the Florida College Financial and Budget Services Office. Once the review is complete, recommendations for edits and amendments are sent to the college to strengthen the proposal. After a second submission and subsequent stringent review by the Division of Florida Colleges, the proposal is submitted with a Division recommendation to approve, deny, or defer to the Commissioner of Education. The Commissioner makes a recommendation to the State Board of Education, which is ultimately responsible for final approval.

The emergence of the workforce baccalaureate degree in the Florida College System has been driven by societal and technological forces and a recognition that higher education must change to remain relevant. The State of Florida has carefully answered the call for innovative yet substantive workforce-oriented baccalaureate programs designed to provide a seamless path from associate degrees to high-demand jobs. By reframing the focus and delivery of select baccalaureates, Florida is helping to lead the nation in maximizing human potential. To remain globally competitive, innovative instructional models as described above demand fresh and

NEW DIRECTIONS FOR COMMUNITY COLLEGES • DOI: 10.1002/cc

forward-thinking, but no less rigorous, views of what truly constitutes quality in teaching and learning.

Growth over the Past Decade

Over the past ten years, the total number of baccalaureate degree programs offered by institutions in the Florida College System has increased dramatically. In 2002, when the first workforce baccalaureate degrees were implemented by community colleges in Florida, there were only three institutions approved to offer a total of fourteen degree programs. These programs were exclusively in the areas of education, nursing, and technology management (Florida College System, 2010). As of 2011 there were nineteen institutions approved to offer 124 workforce-oriented bachelor's degree programs (Florida Department of Education, 2011) that serve over 13,000 students (Bilsky, 2010).

During this same period of time, while the number of workforce baccalaureate degrees offered by FCS institutions were increasing exponentially, it is interesting to note that partnership programs with Florida's public universities and private institutions of higher education were also experiencing rapid growth. Between 2000 and 2010, concurrent-use and joint-use partnerships for baccalaureate and graduate degrees increased by 141 percent (Bilsky, 2010).

Data on baccalaureate headcount enrollment and FTE were first added to the annual Florida Community College System Fact Book in 2005. At that time, only three institutions reported headcount enrollment and FTE for the 2003–2004 reporting period as shown in Table 4.2.

By the 2009–2010 reporting year, fourteen institutions recorded upper-division headcount enrollment and FTE at the levels indicated in Table 4.3 (Florida Department of Education, 2011). Overall, the increase in both system-wide headcount and system-wide enrollment was approximately 900 percent during this six-year period (headcount increase = 894 percent, FTE increase = 904 percent). Nonetheless, upper-division enrollment in the Florida College System represents less than 2 percent of overall system enrollments.

Table 4.2.   Florida College System 2003–2004 Headcount and
FTE by Institution

Institution	Headcount	FTE
Chipola College	13	5.9
Miami Dade College	161	46.5
St. Petersburg College	1,214	542.5
System Total	1,388	594.9

Source: The Fact Book: Report for the Florida Community College System, February 2005.

Table 4.3. Florida College System 2009–2010 Headcount and FTE by Institution

Institution	Headcount	FTE
Broward College	414	128.6
Chipola College	232	134.7
Daytona State College	934	494.6
Edison State College	710	321.5
Florida State College at Jacksonville	816	354.9
Indian River State College	1,558	494.5
State College of Florida, Manatee/Sarasota	46	12.9
Miami Dade College	2,240	907.3
Northwest Florida State College	607	278.0
Palm Beach State College	422	174.4
Polk State College	136	32.3
St. Petersburg College	4,486	1,971.4
Santa Fe College	181	67.4
Seminole State College	26	4.6
System Total	12,408	5,377.1

Source: Florida Department of Education, 2011.
Note: Headcount figures are for students enrolled in a course.

The range of programmatic offerings expanded during this time to include bachelor's degrees in biology to support regional growth in biotechnology and the life sciences; bachelor's degrees in business to serve rural regions of the state; bachelor's degrees in engineering technology and construction management that were implemented when State University System programs were eliminated; and programs in cardiopulmonary sciences, radiologic and imaging sciences, and interior design that were created to address changing credentialing requirements and employment standards in these sectors.

Issues and Implications

The workforce baccalaureate movement in Florida was driven primarily by unmet, workforce needs in fields with critical demand such as teaching, nursing, and applied technology. Community colleges (with strong associate degree programs, a core of full-time faculty with terminal degrees, and modern facilities) were in a perfect position to leverage their resources toward four-year degree production. Florida's twenty-eight community colleges also had access to, and experience with, a unique student population. These nontraditional students were often prevented from attending public universities and private colleges due to restrictions on time, place, and financial resources. All of these factors were influential in contributing to the rapid growth of workforce baccalaureates in Florida. Nevertheless,

NEW DIRECTIONS FOR COMMUNITY COLLEGES • DOI: 10.1002/cc

there are still many issues that confront practitioners on a daily basis, and there are many aspects of this initiative that warrant serious and ongoing consideration by policymakers in Florida (and other states) where expansion of workforce baccalaureates is being contemplated.

Mission.   What will happen to the traditional community college mission at institutions where workforce baccalaureate degree programs are authorized? This is a valid and important question. In Florida, there has been no perceptible decline in associate degree production, A.A. transfer to public and private institutions, or remedial and adult education programs over the past ten years. In fact, enrollments in these programs have increased dramatically. All institutions in the Florida College System still maintain open-door admission for associate degree and certificate programs. This is required in the legislation that authorizes community colleges to provide workforce-oriented baccalaureate degree programs. This legislation reads, in part:

> A Florida college may not terminate its associate in arts or associate in science degree programs as a result of being authorized to offer one or more baccalaureate degree programs. The Legislature intends that the primary responsibility of a Florida college, including a Florida college that offers baccalaureate degree programs, continues to be the provision of associate degrees that provide access to a university (Florida Statutes, §1007.33, 2010).

Policy.   Legislation provides a safeguard for the traditional community college mission, but other aspects of higher education policy in Florida provide the structure to make these unique programs (and now unique institutions) possible. One feature of workforce baccalaureate degree programs in Florida is that they operate as 2+2, intra-institutional, and inter-institutional articulated programs. This means that students must earn an associate degree before they are admitted to the upper division coursework of a bachelor's degree program. Because institutions in the Florida College System require a two-year associate degree for admission to their baccalaureate programs, it allows them to serve their traditional community college mission while also expanding access to the baccalaureate degree. It allows both for open-door admission at the associate degree level and for appropriate admission criteria to be used for admission to the upper-division. This strict separation between the lower-division and the upper-division is beneficial to students. Students can begin their journey to a four-year degree, regardless of their academic preparation. They earn a credential at the halfway point, which will allow many of them to access employment or advance their careers. Then, via intra- and/or inter-institutional articulation, they can move seamlessly into the upper-division coursework of a baccalaureate degree program. Students in Florida also benefit from differential tuition. By law, lower division courses in the Florida College System are offered at a lower tuition than upper-division courses—even within the same institution.

Academic Integrity and Regional Accreditation.   It is essential that community colleges considering the addition of baccalaureate degree programs carefully design and develop curriculum that fully meets the requirements for bachelor's degrees at other public and private "four-year" institutions within their state. To do otherwise creates both the perception, and the reality, of a "baccalaureate-light," with the potential for disadvantaging students who complete these programs as they move into the workforce and/or graduate school study. In Florida, any proposed baccalaureate degree must comply with all statutes, rules, and policies governing baccalaureate degree programs and instruction, including thirty-six hours of general education coursework as well as adhering to statewide policies governing articulation and transfer. To further ensure programmatic integrity, all states are advised to require Level II Regional Accreditation before a community college can award a bachelor's degree.

Approval Process.   A rigorous review and approval process helps to address any concerns about the quality of new baccalaureate degree programs, as well as the need for expanded access—especially during times of reduced budgetary support for higher education. In Florida, the requirements and content for program proposals were modeled upon the elements required for new baccalaureate degrees within the State University System. Proposals are reviewed by a cross-functional work team at the Department of Education, and recommendations to improve the proposal are sent back to the requesting institution. Ultimately, a final proposal is reviewed by the Chancellor of the Florida College System, who makes a recommendation to approve, deny, or defer the proposal to the Commissioner of Education. Likewise, the Commissioner of Education will review the proposal and recommend approval, denial, or deferral to the State Board of Education, which has the power to act on the new degree proposal. While this process is time-consuming and cumbersome, it does provide a strong demonstration of rigor and, ultimately, it improves the quality of new baccalaureate degree proposals.

Strategic Planning and Partnerships.   Community colleges adding baccalaureate programs are advised to plan strategically and work closely with local businesses and industries and other institutions of higher education in their service region to develop programs that will prepare students to fill *unmet* workforce needs in their local communities and region. Careful consideration must be given to issues of access, program costs, and sustainability, as well as to prospects for long-term viability of the curriculum and the current and future employability of graduates. Communication with other higher education stakeholders helps to alleviate concerns about duplication and competition. In Florida, letters of intent to propose new baccalaureate degree programs are sent to the heads of the State University System, the Independent Colleges and Universities of Florida, and the

Commission on Independent Education. Additionally, institutions in the Florida College System are required to communicate with the other higher education providers in their region before submitting a proposal for a new bachelor's degree.

The workforce baccalaureate movement in Florida has not been without controversy. Some public and private universities in Florida, as well as community colleges choosing to forgo developing baccalaureates, have to varying degrees expressed reservations and even opposition to the workforce baccalaureate movement. Scarce state resources, questions about appropriate system governance, and regional institutional competition have generated debate regarding the growth and proliferation of programs. In 2010, the Florida Legislature established a Higher Education Coordinating Council to study and address baccalaureate degree expansion in Florida and to make recommendations to the legislature regarding the future direction of, and responsibility for, long-term bachelor degree production in the state.

Budget.   In the ten years since Florida authorized baccalaureate degrees at the state's community colleges, a number of different funding scenarios have been implemented with varying degrees of success. Fairly robust state support was enjoyed by the early adopters and sorely missed by those colleges developing programs in more recent years. Policy issues involving start-up costs, the segregation/restriction of baccalaureate-related appropriations and student fee revenues, differential funding for higher and lower cost programs, required levels and types of institutional support, and consistent state funding were ultimately identified and examined as critical issues requiring resolution (J. Holdnak, personal communication, April 11, 2011). The current approach to funding baccalaureate programs in the Florida College System was enacted by the Florida Legislature in 2010. Upper-division FTE is treated the same as lower-division FTE and simply added into the system's Community College Program Fund appropriation. The Florida Legislature also controls the tuition for both lower-division and upper-division credit hours in the Florida College System. For the 2010–2011 academic year, upper-division tuition and fees were approximately $100 per credit hour, or about 11 percent higher than the rate for associate degree programs. In recent years, local businesses and industries have contributed significant dollars to assist colleges with start-up costs for degree programs related to workforce needs.

Results.   It is important to remember that results take time to achieve and must be constantly communicated to policy-makers. In Florida, it took ten years to reach an annual enrollment of more than twelve thousand students (five thousand full-time equivalents) and to produce more than fifteen hundred graduates per year (Florida Department of Education, 2011). Legislative term limits and frequent turnover among both elected and appointed statewide policy leaders drive the imperative to constantly communicate the intent, goals, process, and accomplishments of community colleges offering four-year degrees. Numbers and statistics tell an important story, but the words of actual students whose lives have been changed by these programs are often more influential than quantitative data.

The winner of the Seventh Annual Community College Baccalaureate Association's Essay Contest, Domenic Caloia, from St. Petersburg College, provides a window into the meaning and power of these degree programs for the students who are enrolled in them. He writes,

> When I learned that many state community colleges offer four-year degree programs at rates well below university fees, it was like discovering a map to a secret treasure! For the first time in a long while, I had hope for a better future. I returned to school not knowing what to expect. What I encountered was nothing less than transformational (Caloia, 2011, p. 1).

Conclusion

Over the past ten years, Florida has taken dramatic, unprecedented steps to increase access to baccalaureate-level education via transformation within the former community college system. While still maintaining the historic mission of open-admissions, the system is more broadly addressing the economic and workforce needs of the state by increasing public education options for previously un-served or underserved populations. Challenges for the future include strategic, cost-effective programmatic expansion, despite continuing economic uncertainty, as well as continued attention to delivering learning opportunities that prepare students for employment and/or graduate studies. In doing so, the "redefined" Florida College System will continue to demonstrate authentic dedication to its mission and traditions.

References

Bachelor of Applied Science Degree Task Force. Final Report of Activities. Florida Department of Education Web site, 2006, at www.fldoe.org/cc/students/PDF/taskForceReport.pdf

Bilsky, J. "The Future of Florida: Ensuring Access to Postsecondary Education to Keep Florida Working." Florida Higher Education Coordinating Council Meeting Agenda, December 14, 2010, at www.floridahighereducation.org/meetings/20101214.php

Caloia, D. (2011). "Community Colleges Are Portals of Hope and Transformation." Community College Baccalaureate Association Essay Contest, 2011, at www.accbd.org/essay-contest/essay-winners

Finney, J. E. "State Structures for the Governance of Higher Education: Florida Case Study Summary." Technical Paper prepared for State Structures for the Governance of Higher Education and The California Higher Education Policy Center, Spring 1997, at www.capolicycenter.org/florida/florida.html

Florida College System. "Summary 2002–2010: Baccalaureate Programs Approved by State Board of Education." Author, 2010.

Florida Department of Education. The Fact Book: Report for the Florida Community College System. Florida Department of Education Web site, February 2005, at www.fldoehub.org/CCTCMIS/c/Documents/Fact%20Books/factbk05.pdf

Florida Department of Education. The Fact Book: Report for the Florida College System. Florida Department of Education Web site, 2011, at www.fldoehub.org/CCTCMIS/c/Documents/Fact%20Books/fb2011.pdf

Florida Statutes. §1007.01, 2002.

Florida Statutes. §1007.33, 2002.

Florida Statutes. §1004.73, 2002.

Florida Statutes. §1007.33, 2010.

Tomsho, R. "For college-bound, new barriers to entry." *The Wall Street Journal* Web site, 2008, http://sec.online.wsj.com/article/SB122826544902474353.html

Travis, S. "B Students Face Tough Admissions at Florida Universities." The Palm Beach Post, March 17, 2011, at www.palmbeachpost.com/news/schools/b-students-face-tough-admissions-at-florida-universities-1329314.html reviewed 052612jb

United States Census Bureau. Resident Population-July 2008. United States Census Bureau Web site, 2011, at http://www.census.gov/statab/ranks/rank01.html

United States Census Bureau. The 2011 Statistical Abstract: State Rankings. United States Census Bureau Web site, 2011, www.census.gov/compendia/statab/rankings.html

United States Department of Education, National Center for Education Statistics. Fast Facts. United States Department of Education Web site, 2010, at http://nces.ed.gov/fastfacts/display.asp?id=74

JUDITH BILSKY is the vice president and provost at Florida State College.

IAN NEUHARD is the administrative director of baccalaureate programs for the division of instructional services at Indian River State College.

MARY G. LOCKE is the vice president and provost of instructional services at Indian River State College.

New Directions for Community Colleges • DOI: 10.1002/cc

5

This chapter describes the impact of two workforce baccalaureates of applied technology degrees of South Texas College on higher education access for predominately Hispanic students. The addition of the workforce baccalaureates serves as an example of how such degrees increase participation rates for minority students.

The Applied and Workforce Baccalaureate at South Texas College: Specialized Workforce Development Addressing Economic Development

Juan E. Mejia

South Texas College (STC), created in 1993 as South Texas Community College (STCC), has developed from a concept by visionary leaders in the region to currently offering more than one hundred degree and certificate options for students from the counties of Hidalgo and Starr, including two bachelor of applied technology (B.A.T.) degrees. These specialized baccalaureates were developed in partnership with business and industry as a direct response to regional workforce needs. The degrees, which are in the fields of technology management and computer information technologies, provide higher education access to a predominately Hispanic student population and are therefore contributing to the Texas Higher Education Coordinating Board goals of *Closing the Gaps* by raising higher education participation rates and by increasing the number of students earning bachelor degrees.

Brief College History

Prior to 1993, the area that comprises Hidalgo and Starr Counties was a significant geographic region in the state of Texas, encompassing a population of more than 600,000 people without access to a community college (STC, 2009d). During the 73rd Regular Session of the Texas Legislature, a

New Directions for Community Colleges, no. 158, Summer 2012 © 2012 Wiley Periodicals, Inc.
Published online in Wiley Online Library (wileyonlinelibrary.com) • DOI: 10.1002/cc.20016

Senate bill was introduced and immediately sponsored by a House bill that converted the McAllen extension center of Texas State Technical College–Harlingen to a two-county junior college to serve Hidalgo and Starr Counties (STC, 2009d). This crucial Senate Bill was signed into law by former Governor Ann Richards on September 1, 1993. Governor Richards appointed a community leader from each of the seven districts to serve as a trustee for the only legislatively mandated community college in Texas. STCC opened its doors with approximately one thousand students enrolling during the fall semester, many of whom had camped out the evening before to ensure they would be able to enroll in one of the ten certificate programs being offered. Registration doors opened to applause by students celebrating the chance to be active participants in higher education through the vast amount of opportunities provided by a community college of their own. As additional teaching sites were identified, the community welcomed faculty and staff with standing ovations for fulfilling the commitment to a college-going culture. STCC, as it was known during its infancy, made a concentrated effort to include in its mission the commitment to being responsive to the needs of the community through ongoing partnerships and collaboration with the economic development corporations and chambers of commerce.

Since STC's humble beginnings of one thousand students and ten certificate programs, the College has grown to approximately thirty thousand students and more than one hundred degree and certificate options during the Fall 2010 semester, confirming the institutional commitment to a comprehensive mission and continued service to the students of its two-county district (STC, 2009d).

Challenge and Opportunity

Similar to many community colleges throughout the country, the College ensured that students would have access to certificates and associate degrees leading to employment and associate degrees leading to transfer. This resulted in students who completed certificates and associate of applied science degrees rapidly joining the workforce, and students who completed associate of science or associate of arts degrees successfully transferring to universities of their choice. The challenge identified by leaders from the community and validated by the college leadership team focused on graduates who were interested in continuing their education post completion of an associate of applied science degree. These already successful students who had graduated from the community college, attained employment, and were now ready for upward mobility and supervisory opportunities in their career field were experiencing a type of "glass ceiling" because of the missing baccalaureate degree.

The initial option was to partner with regional universities through articulation agreements to provide an academic pathway for these gradu-

NEW DIRECTIONS FOR COMMUNITY COLLEGES • DOI: 10.1002/cc

ates and now returning students; however, the completion of a baccalaureate degree through this pathway would require that the students enroll in a large number of leveling courses, which was discouraging, time consuming, and very costly to the student, the employer, the community, and to the state. Another possible solution was to partner with an institution of higher learning which might have a type of bachelor of applied science or a bachelor of applied arts and science degree, so that students would be able to transfer a greater amount of credits. At times, these degrees were a type of catch-all approach, without a specific focus on student learning outcomes leading to value added and competency building. According to Keith Patridge, President of the McAllen Economic Development Corporation, leaders from business and industry review and assess the educational attainment level for the region when deciding where to establish a company or plant (McAllen Chamber of Commerce, 2011). It is vitally important that a company be assured that the region has a workforce that is appropriately educated and trained.

Genesis of the Applied and Workforce Baccalaureate

The founding president of the college, Dr. Shirley A. Reed, promised city leaders in the district that the college would never lose sight of the importance of being responsive to their needs, and she challenged the college community to explore ways to remove the glass ceiling for the many students who had completed their associate of applied science degrees, and to continue until those students were gainfully employed and ready to take on supervisory or management roles in their organizations. The powerful ingredient to be added was to ensure that the degree would not be merely the attainment of a piece of paper, but would have the value that comes from a specialized degree with the appropriate academic rigor, leading to increased skill-sets, through student learning outcomes infused throughout the curriculum, and the ability to withstand the test of key performance indicators such as enrollment, persistence, subsequent course success, graduation, employment upward mobility, and pathway to a graduate degree.

At the state level, the *Closing the Gaps 2015* educational initiative, along with the changing needs of local employers and the lack of access to baccalaureate degrees for nontraditional students, opened the doors to explore the baccalaureate movement in Texas. In 2002, education leaders of several community colleges in Texas began exploring the possibility of offering these specialized baccalaureate degrees.

Ongoing Leadership by the Legislature

Great credit belongs to the Texas Legislature when during its 78th Regular Session of 2003 a number of bills were filed to amend the Texas Education

Code to authorize the awards beyond an associate degree at community colleges (SB 286, 2003). These amendments allowed the governor to sign a bill establishing a pilot project that allowed three select community colleges to each offer up to five baccalaureate degrees in the fields of applied science and applied technology (SB 286, 2003). Brazosport College, Midland College, and South Texas Community College were selected by the legislature to participate in this pilot (SB 286, 2003). The Texas Legislature asked the Texas Higher Education Coordinating Board to provide leadership and support to the three community colleges with direction that:

1. The community colleges would stay true to the comprehensive mission of community colleges.
2. Each participating community college met the requirements of Level II accreditation set by the Commission on Colleges of the Southern Association of Colleges and Schools.
3. Each respective institution was allowed to offer up to five baccalaureate degrees in applied science and applied technology fields.
4. Evidence of need would be demonstrated for the proposed degree program in the region.
5. The applied degrees would not duplicate programs offered by the area universities.
6. Each community college demonstrated the ability to support the new programs, facilities, faculty, administration, and libraries.
7. Each college entered into articulation agreements with other senior institutions so students might continue their education at other institutions if the pilot project ended.

As part of the guidelines by the Southern Association of Colleges and Schools (SACS) at that time, South Texas Community College was asked to remove the term *community* from its name; it became the institution known today as South Texas College. In 2005, the Texas Higher Education Coordinating Board approved the offering of the bachelor of applied technology degree in technology management and the college met all conditions for Level II, baccalaureate granting privileges, from SACS.

It is important to note that during the 80th Regular Session of the Texas Legislature, a house bill was introduced and signed into law by Governor Rick Perry on June 15, 2007, which further amended the Texas Education Code and removed the pilot status of the applied baccalaureate program (HB 2198, 2007). It did not, however, expand the program beyond the original three community colleges or remove the aforementioned conditions imposed by the original senate bill (HB 2198, 2007). The legislature also requested that the participating community colleges prepare biennial reports on the operation and effectiveness of the programs being offered (HB 2198, 2007).

Technology Management

The bachelor of applied technology in technology management coursework is balanced between practical training and working with real-life projects that enhance the educational experiences for students. The breadth of the coursework enables each graduate to lead and manage by utilizing a wide variety of business, finance, technology, and human resources development skills. The degree prepares the graduate to:

- Supervise and manage the financial operations of a business
- Utilize management and motivational theories to enhance the performance of employees and work-teams
- Use project and quality management strategies to successfully manage and secure organizational resources
- Apply oral and written communication skills and leverage technology to enhance communications
- Manage the organization or the business unit within legal and ethical boundaries
- Employ creative and critical thinking processes to resolve problems of the business unit
- Use appropriate electronic commerce strategies to enhance profitability of the organization
- Exhibit analytical thought, informed judgment, ethical behavior, and an appreciation for diversity
- Utilize appropriate information technology systems to enhance organizational performance
- Understand the challenges involved in conducting international business and its impact on the future growth of the organization

The Fall 2005 semester had an official enrollment of forty students in the newly approved applied baccalaureate program. Table 5.1 demonstrates how the annual unduplicated enrollment in upper-division courses has continued to increase over the years for a 548 percent enrollment increase in six years.

Computer and Information Technologies

During the Fall 2007 semester, the bachelor of applied technology in computer and information technologies was launched. This degree is designed

Table 5.1.   Enrollment Chart

Academic Year	2005–2006	2006–2007	2007–2008	2008–2009	2009–2010	2010–2011
Technology Management	40	112	186	245	252	259

NEW DIRECTIONS FOR COMMUNITY COLLEGES • DOI: 10.1002/cc

Table 5.2.   Enrollment Chart

Academic Year	2007–2008	2008–2009	2009–2010	2010–2011
Computer and Information Technologies	58	97	117	132

to prepare students for successful careers in the wide variety of information technology fields. The coursework is balanced between theoretical and technical competencies associated with CIT to prepare graduates for a number of demands placed on these professionals (STC, 2009b). The degree is designed to educate and train students with relevant, technical knowledge of related practices to provide solutions for real-world problems as well as to provide technical support for computer-based information systems. As shown in Table 5.2, a total of fifty-eight students enrolled in Fall 2007 and since then the enrollment has increased by 128 percent over four years.

The combined student demographics for the programs include a gender split of 41 percent female and 59 percent male, with 92 percent of the students being Hispanic, 4 percent white non-Hispanic, 1 percent black, and 3 percent other. The breakdown for enrollment status is 56 percent full time and 44 percent part time.

The fall-to-fall persistence rates for the Technology Management degree since fall 2005 have remained strong with a range from 85 percent to 93 percent, and 85 percent to 90 percent for the computer and information technologies degree.

With the college having a strong focus on *College Going and College Graduation,* the two baccalaureate degree programs at STC have prepared 361 graduates with placement/employment rates close to 90 percent for each respective program.

From the Students

The College's Research and Analytical Services Office conducted an analysis of the Bachelor of Applied Technology Exit Survey in 2009. This Exit Survey was administered to provide recent graduates an opportunity to evaluate their experiences and impressions of the program and to provide information to help understand the development of students as well as their opinions concerning their educational experiences. The results of the survey were consistently positive across all areas of inquiry. When asked "If you could take college over, would you select the same program you are completing?" 95 percent of respondents answered "yes," and an overwhelming majority shared they were very satisfied with their programs (STC, 2009a).

A Culture of Evidence

Since its inception in fall of 2005, the bachelor of applied technology program's rates of enrollment and graduation have grown exponentially, making it evident that there is a need for additional baccalaureates of this type at STC. To ensure that the current programs are of the highest quality, this study was designed collaboratively by Research and Analytical Services (RAS) and the Bachelor of Applied Technology Division to measure the satisfaction with the program by the graduates of the program. There are four areas of inquiry: employment or status after graduation, satisfaction with instruction, satisfaction with student-faculty interaction, and satisfaction with mentoring. Out of seventy-five students in the graduating class at the time, sixty-eight completed the online exit survey during the months of April and May of 2009 (STC, 2009a). Four surveys were excluded because they were incomplete yielding a response rate of 85 percent (sixty-four out of seventy-five) (STC, 2009a).

Purpose of Study

The survey was designed to serve two purposes: to give recent graduates an opportunity to evaluate and express their experiences and impressions of the programs; and to provide information to help STC understand the development of students as well as their opinions concerning their educational experiences while enrolled.

Methodology

The survey design was conducive to the research methodology, leading the respondent from general to very specific questions. Analyses were also conducted in that order. First, percent of frequencies for polar (yes/no) questions were analyzed. Likert-type scale questions were then analyzed by looking at the frequencies of levels of agreement and scale means by giving each of these levels a number value (Strongly Agree = 4, Agree = 3, Disagree = 2, and Strongly Disagree = 1). Finally, these scale questions were grouped by area of inquiry and levels of agreement and scale means were analyzed.

Research Questions

The research questions included, but were not limited to, the following: Are the graduates employed, and/or what are their impressions of the programs relative to employment? Are they satisfied with the instruction they received while in the program? Are they satisfied with the level of interaction with program faculty? Are the faculty from the program supportive in offering guidance to their students? (See Table 5.3).

NEW DIRECTIONS FOR COMMUNITY COLLEGES • DOI: 10.1002/cc

Table 5.3.   Employment or Status after Graduation

	Yes
Are you currently employed?	93.5%
Did having coursework from STC help you get your current job?	54.8%
Did the coursework from STC help you to improve your current job?	93.5%
Do you expect to change jobs based on your B.A.T. degree from STC?	75.8%
Do you currently have a job offer?	24.2%
Do you expect to receive a promotion based on your B.A.T. degree from STC?	59.7%
Did the education you received in the bachelor programs meet your expectations?	91.8%

Key Findings

Because of the overall positive responses likely due to the self-selected responsiveness of the students in the program, linear relationships between any of the questions on the survey were disregarded as unreliable due to the positive skew or right-skewed distribution.

Employment or Status Following Graduation

Results from the survey indicate that 94 percent of the recent bachelor of applied technology graduates who responded were currently employed (STC, 2009c). Furthermore, 94 percent agreed that course work from STC helped them to improve their current job, while 92 percent believed the education they received from their program met their expectations, and 95 percent concurred that they would re-enroll in the same program if they had to do it again (STC, 2009a). Accordingly, this high satisfaction level suggests that these students believe that their educational and related occupational expectations were achieved. Based on their degree attainment, 78 percent were confident that they expected to change jobs (STC, 2009a). While 62 percent responded that they had plans to enroll in a graduate level program, 60 percent of the respondents specified the name of the graduate school they planned to attend in the follow-up comment question (e.g., Baylor University, Lamar University, Sam Houston State University, Texas A&M University, and The University of Texas) (STC, 2009a).

Therefore, it is apparent that having attained a four-year degree is an incentive to acquire a graduate-level degree.

Instruction.   For all three of the instruction-related questions, the majority (96 percent) of graduates responded (with responses of "Strongly Agree" and "Agree") that they believe that they received a well-delivered and quality education (see Table 5.4).

Student-Faculty Interaction

This area of inquiry earned the highest percentage of agreement (97 percent). All of the graduates (100 percent) agreed that "There was good com-

Table 5.4.   Likert Scale Questions by Area of Inquiry

Likert Scale Questions by Area of Inquiry	% Strongly Agree/Agree	4-Point Scale Mean
Instruction		
Courses listed in the degree plans are offered frequently enough for timely completion of degree requirements.	95.0%	3.37
The courses I took were well-taught.	98.4%	3.38
Faculty members were well-qualified to teach their courses.	95.0%	3.40
Aggregate	96.1%	3.38
Student–Faculty Interaction		
There was good communication between faculty and students regarding student needs.	96.6%	3.60
There was good communication between faculty and students regarding concerns.	95.0%	3.55
There was good communication between faculty and students regarding suggestions.	100.0%	3.63
There were many opportunities outside the classroom for interaction between students and faculty.	96.7%	3.57
Aggregate	97.1%	3.59
Mentoring		
Faculty were helpful and supportive in my search for professional employment.	86.7%	3.23
Faculty were willing to meet with me to discuss my academic performance.	98.3%	3.55
Aggregate	92.5%	3.39

munication between faculty and students regarding suggestions," and 97 percent were in agreement that faculty were well qualified to teach the courses (STC, 2009a).

The majority also agreed that there were opportunities outside the classroom to meet with faculty members about their needs and concerns.

Mentoring

As mentioned earlier, a large proportion of these graduates were immediately employed. Comparatively, it is worth noting that a near-equal proportion (87 percent) indicated that "Faculty were helpful and supportive" when they searched for employment (STC, 2009a).

Virtually all of the respondents (98 percent) believed that "faculty were willing" to take the time to discuss their academic performance. Key findings revealed that 94 percent of graduates are employed, 100 percent of graduates agree that there is good communication between faculty and students, 98 percent of graduates believe that "faculty were willing" to take the time to discuss their academic performance, and 95 percent would re-enroll in the same program if they had to do it again (STC, 2009b).

NEW DIRECTIONS FOR COMMUNITY COLLEGES • DOI: 10.1002/cc

Employer Feedback

The college also conducts an employer satisfaction survey and collected data from employers whose contact information had been voluntarily provided by STC graduates in the graduate follow-up survey or from employers serving on program advisory boards. The objective was to utilize employer feedback to improve existing or develop new policies to match learning outcomes with the workforce needs (STC, 2009c). In addition to the distribution of the findings, they can also be found posted on the college Web site: Employer Satisfaction with STC Graduates Research Brief (STC, 2009c) at http://isp.southtexascollege.edu/ras/research/pdf/Research %20Brief%20-%20Employer%20Satisfaction%20Survey.pdf.

Conclusion

The comprehensive mission of South Texas College celebrates a commitment to serving the students and communities of south Texas through quality academic programs, supported by innovative strategies from the strong division of student affairs and enrollment management. The board of trustees, the college president, and all faculty and staff are proud stakeholders in a community college that has not only been reactive, but most importantly proactive regarding the needs from business and industry, while listening to the voices of students and graduates. The workforce baccalaureate is key to strong economic development for the region of south Texas, for the state, and for the country while competing in a global economy.

References

HB 2198, 80th Session, Texas, 2007.

McAllen Chamber of Commerce. (2011). "Education." Retrieved from www.mcallen. org/pdf/profile/Education.pdf

SB 286, 78th Session, Texas, 2003.

South Texas College. "An Analysis of the Bachelor of Applied Technology (BAT) Exit Survey 2009." South Texas College Web site, 2009a, at http://isp.southtexascollege. edu/ras/research/pdf/BAT%20Graduate%20Exit%20Survey%20-%20revised.pdf

South Texas College. "Bachelor of Applied Technology in Computer & Information Technologies: Mission Statement." South Texas College Web site, 2009b, at http:// ms.southtexascollege.edu/computerscience/bat-cit.

South Texas College. "Employer Satisfaction with South Texas College (STC) Graduates." South Texas College Web site, 2009c, at http://isp.southtexascollege.edu/ras/ research/pdf/Research%20Brief%20-%20Employer%20Satisfaction%20Survey.pdf

South Texas College. "History." South Texas College Web site, 2009d, at www. southtexascollege.edu/about/history.html/index.html

JUAN E. MEJIA is the vice president for academic affairs at South Texas College.

NEW DIRECTIONS FOR COMMUNITY COLLEGES • DOI: 10.1002/cc

6

This chapter describes the results of case study research on the transfer of learning from the classroom to the cooperative education workplace and includes recommendations for curriculum changes to improve the transfer of learning.

The Work Experience Component of an Ontario College Baccalaureate Program

Marguerite M. Donohue, Michael L. Skolnik

Community colleges in Canada began offering baccalaureate programs in the 1990s. Presently community colleges in four of the five largest provinces of Canada are eligible to submit applications to the relevant government ministry or agency for baccalaureate programs. We estimate that about 135 baccalaureate programs are now being offered in thirty-two colleges across Canada, which include about sixty programs in twelve colleges just in Ontario. All of the baccalaureate programs in community colleges are in applied areas of study with workforce preparation as the principal goal (Skolnik, 2001).

Typically, baccalaureate programs in Canadian community colleges are "applied" also in regard to the way that learning is fostered. Like the diploma programs that the colleges offer in related or similar fields, the baccalaureate programs emphasize inductive more than deductive learning, and make considerable use of experiential learning and learning-by-doing. In many cases, a period of paid work experience is a requirement of these programs. In Ontario, the requirement for baccalaureate programs in colleges is for eight semesters of classroom study plus a minimum of one paid work term of at least fourteen weeks. This requirement for a paid work term reinforces the importance placed on practical application of theoretical learning in these Ontario degree programs.

Because of the emphasis that community college baccalaureate programs place on experiential learning, and on the integration of classroom and workplace-based learning, it is important that these two arenas of

New Directions for Community Colleges, no. 158, Summer 2012 © 2012 Wiley Periodicals, Inc.
Published online in Wiley Online Library (wileyonlinelibrary.com) • DOI: 10.1002/cc.20017

learning be effectively connected in curriculum planning and program delivery. One aspect of this relationship involves the transfer of learning from the classroom to the workplace setting. This chapter reports the findings of an in-depth study of such transfer of learning in a baccalaureate program in one community college in Ontario. The study involved an analysis of the relationship between transfer of learning and various curriculum, workplace, and personal characteristics of learners such as preferred learning style (Donohue, 2010). Programs with a work experience component of the type described in this chapter are generally referred to in Ontario as cooperative education programs, and that term is used here in referring to the program that was the subject of the study.

Research Questions

The purpose of this research study was to examine the extent of transfer of learning from the classroom to the cooperative education workplace in the bachelor of applied business program at a large, multi-campus, comprehensive college of applied arts and technology in Ontario and the relationship between the students' learning styles and the transfer of learning. Four research questions were used to guide this research: What is the extent of the transfer of learning from the classroom to the cooperative education workplace in the bachelor of applied business program? What are the differences in the types of learning outcomes that students with differing learning styles transfer from the classroom to the cooperative education workplace? What are the enablers and barriers to transfer of learning identified by the students, and are there differences depending on the student's learning style? What planned learning is in place in the program's curriculum to promote transfer of learning from the classroom to the cooperative education workplace?

Recognizing that each student brings unique characteristics pertaining to learning to their educational experience, this research study incorporated Kolb's (1984) learning styles as a means of exploring the relationship that an individual's learning style may have with the transfer of learning. Kolb's experiential learning theory was used as the theoretical construct grounding this research. Specifically, Kolb's learning cycle of concrete experience, observation and reflection, formation of abstract concepts, and then testing the concepts in new situations was the framework used to examine the transfer of the knowledge and skills learned in the classroom to the cooperative education workplace. In contrast to the studies by Grosjean (2000) and Milley (2004) this study focused on the transfer of learning from the classroom to the cooperative education workplace.

Literature Review

The literature review explores the research related to cooperative education. It also discusses Kolb's experiential learning theory and learning styles with a focus on the educational context.

NEW DIRECTIONS FOR COMMUNITY COLLEGES • DOI: 10.1002/cc

Cooperative Education.   Cooperative (co-op) education became part of higher education in the early 20th century. Proponents of this educational model have touted the benefits it provides the students, such as experience in the world of work, job search skills, employability skills such as communication and teamwork skills, and help in establishing career direction (Canadian Council on Learning, 2008; Milne, 2007). A defining characteristic of cooperative education is that students are engaged in productive real life work (Ryder, 1987) that provides them with the opportunity to integrate the knowledge, attitudes, and skills they learn in the classroom with a practical workplace experience (Apostolides and Looye, 1997; Eames, 2000; Stark, 2004; Weisz and Kimber, 2001). By providing them with opportunities to explore the world beyond the classroom, cooperative education prepares students to make a smooth transition from college or university to the workplace.

There are three stages in the co-op experience: planning, the work experience itself, and evaluation/reflection. Pedagogical approaches such as co-op courses, workshops, seminars, and one-on-one advising are most commonly used to prepare students for co-op. Traditional co-op programs alternate between academic semesters and co-op work terms beginning after either the first or second term, thus extending the length of time that students are in postsecondary education.

Several recent studies of co-op programs examined the learning experience as it relates to the cooperative education work experience (Davidge-Johnston, 1996; Grosjean, 2000; Milley, 2004; Stark, 2004). These studies focused predominantly on what the authors called essential skills—that is, the communication skills, organizational skills, job interviewing skills, and job search skills learned during the cooperative education workplace experience. In reporting their results, the authors indicated having observed some transfer of knowledge and skills from the classroom to the workplace and vice versa. However, the conclusions drawn by these researchers indicated a need to further examine the link between classroom learning and the cooperative education workplace learning experience.

Saltmarsh (1992) suggested that for cooperative education to play a meaningful role in higher education a shift away from a structural approach towards relating theory to practice was necessary. Others who recognized the importance of strengthening the connection between the learning in the classroom and the workplace have found experiential learning theory, and the many learning theories that have developed from it, useful as theoretical frameworks for cooperative education research (Johnston, Angerilli, and Gajdamaschko, 2004; Ricks, Van Gyn, Branton, Cutt, Loken, and Ney, 1990; Van Gyn, 1996).

Experiential Learning Theory.   Kolb's (1984) experiential learning theory was developed using the strengths of Dewey's experiential learning theory, Piaget's cognitive development theory, and Lewin's group dynamics and action research model. He believed that for students, "field placement

NEW DIRECTIONS FOR COMMUNITY COLLEGES • DOI: 10.1002/cc

or work/study is an empowering experience that allows them to capitalize on practical strengths while testing the application of ideas discussed in the classroom" (p. 6). He contended that this type of experiential learning provided a link between education and work that increased the relevance of higher education.

Kolb (1984) described learning as a process that occurred when there was interplay between expectation and experience. He contended that learning was a continuous process grounded in experience; that all learning was relearning; and that learning was by its nature a conflict-filled process. Brew (1993) built on Kolb's definition and described learning as "grasping or getting hold of or possessing something we did not previously have, or changing an aspect of our view of the world" (p. 93). Boud, Cohen, and Walker (1993) stressed that "learning required interaction, either directly or symbolically, with elements outside the learner. It is only by counterposing experience with something which is internal to the learner that meaning can be created" (p. 2).

Kolb stated that new knowledge, skills, or attitudes were achieved by movement through the four stages of experiential learning with each stage reflecting an adapting learning mode (learning abilities). He suggested that learners should go through the cycle from *concrete experience* (learning through experiencing or feeling) which provides the basis for *reflective observation* (learning through experiencing or feeling). These observations are then converted to *abstract conceptualizations* (learning through explaining or thinking) that lead to implications for action through *active experimentation* (learning through applying or doing) in new experiences. He contended that all four stages must be completed for a complete learning experience to take place. Kolb described this four-stage learning cycle as becoming a spiral when what was learned in one experience was used in the next learning experience, and so on. Vince (1998) described the learning cycle as "an accessible way of expressing both the importance of experiential knowledge and the link between theory and practice" (p. 306).

Kolb's concept of learning styles "describes individual differences in learning based on the learner's preference for employing different phases of the learning cycle" (Kolb and Kolb, 2005, pp. 194–195). The divergent learning style relies primarily on concrete experience and reflective observation (looking at things from a variety of perspectives and using information from their senses and feelings). The assimilative learning style relies primarily on abstract conceptualization and reflective observation (using inductive reasoning and creating theoretical models). The convergent learning style relies primarily on the dominant learning abilities of abstract conceptualization and active experimentation (solving problems and finding solutions to practical issues). The accommodative learning style relies on concrete experience and active experimentation (getting things done and getting involved in new experiences) (Chapman, 2006; Kolb, 1984, 2005; Raschick, Maypole, and Day, 1998). This model offers a way to understand an individual's learning style while also providing an explanation of the cycle of experiential learning that applies to all of us (Chapman, 2006).

As a result of heredity, life experience, educational specialization, professional career choice, current job role, and present environment, most people will develop a clear preference for a particular learning style. The ability to switch between styles does not come easily to many people. Where a strong learning style preference exists, learning will be most effective if learning is oriented to that preference (Chapman, 2006; Kolb, 1984).

Kolb (1984) maintained that teaching and learning in higher education, in order to foster student development, needed to take into consideration the individual learning styles of students. Other aspects of the educational system that influence the learning process also need to be managed. He contended that many techniques were used to assist the learning process, but the weakness of nearly all of these was their failure to recognize and explicitly provide for the differences in learning styles of both individuals and subject matters (p. 196).

Methodology

This research used case study methodology and both qualitative and quantitative research tools to gather data to address the research questions. Taking part in the study was a purposive convenience sample of students from the third year of the bachelor of applied business program at a large comprehensive college, who had completed the second of three cooperative education work terms in the program. Six of twenty-one (28.6 percent) eligible students agreed to participate and completed all components of the study. The cooperative education work experience occurs in alternate terms beginning after the fourth academic semester. Students in this program are required to successfully complete all courses in the program of study that preceded each cooperative education work term in order to be eligible to participate in that work term.

The learning examined in this research was defined as the course learning outcomes (CLOs), as articulated in the course outlines of all the courses taken by the students prior to the second cooperative education workplace experience (i.e., specifically, the learning from the first five of eight academic semesters). The CLOs were categorized as either an application of concept or application of skill. The categorization of the CLOs was validated by the program coordinator. The categorization of the CLOs aligned with two of Kolb's four learning modes: application of concepts aligned with abstract conceptualization, and application of skills aligned with active experimentation (Kolb, 1984). Individuals with assimilating and converging learning styles have more of a tendency toward using abstract conceptualization (i.e., thinking), while individuals with accommodating and converging learning styles have more of a tendency toward active experimentation (i.e., doing).

NEW DIRECTIONS FOR COMMUNITY COLLEGES • DOI: 10.1002/cc

The self-selected participants first completed the Kolb Learning Style Inventory (LSI), an instrument developed to enable individuals to identify their learning style preference. It "is designed to help you understand how you learn best in educational settings and everyday life situations" (Kolb, 2005, p. 2). They then completed a researcher-developed course learning outcomes questionnaire comprised of 134 CLOs from the courses taken prior to the second co-op work term. Following this, they participated in a one-on-one interview with the researcher that lasted about thirty minutes. After the interview, participants were provided with their individual results of the LSI, an explanation of the results, as well as Kolb's interpretive booklet about the LSI. The five separate co-op documents completed by the student, the employer supervisor, and the co-op staff member during the second co-op work term were collected for analysis by the researcher. Using several different methodologies or sources to collect relevant data was important to triangulate the data (Flick, 1992; Johnson, 1997).

Data collected using each of these methods were validated as appropriate, triangulated, and analyzed to develop the results, analyses, and the conclusions presented later in this chapter. These results were presented in the aggregate so as to protect the anonymity of the participants as outlined in the Letter of Informed Consent.

Self-reporting was identified as a limitation in this study. Students were asked to complete a questionnaire consisting of 134 items and participate in an interview relating to experiences that occurred up to two years previously. They also self-selected which may have resulted in an overrepresentation of participants who had positive experiences that they wanted to share. Future studies of this nature could consider using fewer items in a questionnaire and having participants use a desk diary or a similar reporting tool during the co-op experience.

Findings and Analysis

The research findings and analyses are presented in response to the four research questions.

Research Question 1: What is the extent of the transfer of learning from the classroom to the cooperative education program in the bachelor of applied business program? Close to 74 percent (99 of 134) of the CLOs from the courses studied prior to the second co-op workplace experience were reported as used by at least one participant, were used at least once or used regularly by all participants, or were reported as used by a majority of participants during that co-op experience. The CLOs reported as used by all of the participants in this study (8 percent of the CLOs) were clustered in the first two semesters. These CLOs describe technical and communication skills. The CLOs reported as used by the majority of the participants (19.4 percent of the CLOs) were also concentrated in the first two semesters. These CLOs relate to fundamental business concepts. Analysis of the interview transcripts revealed that the participants predominantly identified concepts related to the field of business, with some mention of more specific skills related to e-business supply chain management. They also described using technical and communication skills. One item mentioned by five of the six participants was learning related to teamwork as illustrated in the following student quote.

> There are a lot of group projects in our class . . . we had a lot of group meetings, obviously a lot of brainstorming, a lot of exchange of ideas . . . and at the same time a lot of conflict resolution . . . I used the same strategy back at work. My co-op placement is very team-oriented; it's a project management area so there is a lot of collaboration, a lot of team work, a lot of reviewing each other's work.

This is consistent with several of the factors explored by Johnston and colleagues (2004). One factor they reported was: "co-op derives classic employability outcomes . . . providing outcomes such as communication skills, teamwork skills, problem solving, and job finding" (Johnston, Angerilli, and Gajdamaschko, 2004, pp. 176–177). Another factor they described was: "co-op is for the application of school learned skills to the workplace . . . is the only factor that clearly sees the role of school as teaching the relevant technical skills of a discipline and the role of co-op as providing the opportunity to apply those school-derived skills in the real world" (Johnston, Angerilli, and Gajdamaschko, 2004, pp. 178–179). This factor also supports "the notion of skills transfer between school and work" (Johnston, Angerilli, and Gajdamaschko, 2004, pp. 178–179).

Examination of the pattern of CLO use over the five academic semesters in this program showed decreasing reported use of CLOs as the participants progressed through the semesters. Almost all of the CLOs from Semesters 01 and 02 were reported as used (100 percent and 94.7 percent, respectively). In aggregate, the participants reported using approximately three quarters of the CLOs in Semesters 03 and 04 (72.9 percent and 75 percent, respectively). CLO use reported in Semester 05 dropped to 29.2 percent. If either recency of learning or recall had an impact on responses to the course learning outcomes questionnaire, higher levels of reported use of CLOs in the more recent semesters might have been reported. When the CLOs were examined, it became clear that those used in earlier semesters were more broadly applicable, while those from courses in higher semesters were more specific.

Research Question 2: What are the differences in the types of learning outcomes that students with differing learning styles transfer from the classroom to the cooperative education workplace? Two of the six participants demonstrated a preference for the assimilating learning style, and four demonstrated a preference for the accommodating learning style. Kolb (1984) compared career classifications to the learning styles delineated in his experiential learning theory. He demonstrated, through his research and the research of others, that career classifications could be oriented on the experiential learning

NEW DIRECTIONS FOR COMMUNITY COLLEGES • DOI: 10.1002/cc

theory framework. Relevant to this research study, business and organizational type careers were positioned in the accommodating learning style quadrant. Science and general culture type careers were positioned in the assimilating learning style quadrant (pp. 128–131). Loo's (2002) meta-analytic review of eight studies of business students, with a combined sample size of 1,791, showed a higher proportion of assimilating learning style students and a lower proportion of accommodating learning style students than would be expected if learning styles were equally distributed. Kolb (1984) stated that not all individuals within a particular career type have the same learning style, nor should they be expected to. That Loo's results were counter to Kolb's findings with respect to the learning style of individuals in the field of business supports the notion of individuality but puts into question the particular learning style that individuals in the field of business may tend to have. That not all students in this study had the same learning style reinforces Kolb's contention that not all individuals in a particular career type have the same learning style.

Analysis of the findings related to transfer of learning from the classroom to the cooperative education workplace with respect to the participants' learning styles revealed that the accommodating and assimilating learning style groups in this case appeared to be more similar than they were different. As a group, the accommodating learning style group all used only one CLO. The assimilating learning style group did not all use any of the CLOs. Neither group seemed to favor using one type of application over the other, that is, application of concept or application of skill. The small sample size and the uneven distribution of learning styles prevented statistical analysis regarding this part of the question.

Research Question 3: What are the enablers and barriers to transfer of learning identified by the students? Are there differences in enablers and/or barriers depending on the student's learning style? Four summary statements were developed based on the analysis of the co-op documentation and the participants' descriptions of what enabled them to transfer learning from the classroom to the cooperative education workplace: developing a plan to use the knowledge and skills learned in the classroom in the co-op workplace; having the opportunity to use the knowledge and skills learned in the classroom in the co-op workplace; working in an environment that is supportive and provides breadth and depth of experience for co-op students; and experiencing a positive change in self-perception. The following is an example of an enabling circumstance described by a student:

> As [the co-op experience] evolved and as everybody got a little more comfortable with it, I got to learn more and more, and I got some opportunities that maybe would not have been standard for a first time around [co-op student], so that was a bonus.

The participants identified fewer barriers to transfer of learning from the classroom to the cooperative education workplace than enablers. Two

New Directions for Community Colleges • DOI: 10.1002/cc

summary statements represent these barriers: working in a co-op position that is specialized, e.g., "Our program is so broad, covering so many different topics, but in my second co-op term, it was a very specialized thing that I was doing, so there was a lot of learning that I didn't get an opportunity to apply"; and dealing with organizational factors such as issues related to payroll and restructuring, e.g., "During my co-op, my boss got laid off. That was a little weird . . . I did a project and we were going to implement it, but my boss had to be involved to implement it. He was gone the next day so I didn't get to implement it."

All of the enablers and barriers to transfer of learning identified in this research study were reflective of the workplace culture and authentic learning experience variables identified by Beckett and Hager (2000). The other three variables that influence workplace learning that they found—that is, quality of learning materials, role of language and literacy, and company/business size—were not revealed clearly in this study.

The summary statements describing the enablers and barriers to transfer of learning derived from the information gathered in the documentation and the interviews in this research study reflect the kinds of things that these participants felt were either necessary or missing to help them take what they had learned in the classroom and use it to further their learning in the cooperative education workplace.

Research Question 4: What planned learning is in place in the program's curriculum to promote transfer of learning from the classroom to the cooperative education workplace? The course outlines for Co-op Work Terms I and II provided clear links between classroom learning and the workplace, with all of the CLOs and the majority of the embedded knowledge and skills linked in some way to transfer of learning. However, the academic course outlines provided no tangible evidence of the professors' intent to link classroom learning with the co-op workplace or vice versa. The work term learning plan, in which the students, in conjunction with the employer supervisor, describe what they plan to learn during the co-op experience, is a key first step as they begin their co-op work term experience. Including this as a requirement for the co-op work terms is consistent with the recommendations in the literature. Cheek and Campbell (1994) emphasized that "purposeful activity linked to newly acquired behaviors will facilitate the transfer of learning" (p. 27). Eakins (2000) concluded from her research that it was important to seek "an approach to structuring the workplace context and the curriculum of cooperative education so as to support applied learning in the workplace" (p. 63).

When the participants were asked about their experience in the classroom it was apparent that, at least to some minimal extent, their experience in co-op was brought back to the classroom. However, with the exception of the Co-op Work Term course outlines, there is little evidence to show that the curriculum was designed to help the students transfer the knowledge and skills they learned in the classroom to the cooperative education workplace. That students felt this disconnect is illustrated in the following quote from one of the participants:

> . . . one of the things about learning classroom-type things is that it sort of works on the theory, and sort of presents a very perfect ideal of how things should be, whereas when you get out into the workplace, things don't necessarily happen in the perfect theoretical way. Again, there are these hidden surprises, individuals, or structures that just get in the way of applying the knowledge.

Research Conclusions

The researcher drew several conclusions from the analysis of the findings. First, foundation skills learned in the classroom, such as communication and technical skills, and in this case general business concepts, are used in all of the cooperative education workplace experiences in this study. The results showed that students in this program used what they learned in the classroom during their co-op workplace experience and support the importance of broad-based communication and technical skills, as well as general business concepts in the curriculum.

Second, the co-op work term experience itself, including the workplace environment and culture, is more important than the student's learning style in explaining the learning from the classroom that a student is able to transfer to the co-op workplace. Aside from the commonly used CLOs, the CLOs used by the individual participants were clearly related to different but specific areas within the field of e-business supply chain management. The differences in the CLOs used among all of the students were related to the opportunities to use CLOs during the particular co-op work term experience, the culture and environment of the workplace, and the supportiveness of the employer supervisor, rather than the learning style of the student. The learning that students transfer from the classroom is dependent on the position that a student obtains for his or her cooperative education workplace experience. Some jobs provide for a more focused experience; others provide more breadth. The small sample size may have influenced the findings related to this conclusion.

Third, co-op experiences may not challenge students to the level they may be capable of attaining with respect to what they have learned in class. The low level of reported use of the CLOs in the higher academic levels, particularly those that represent higher level concepts and skills, is an indication that these students were not necessarily working to their potential related to what they had learned to date in the classroom. This has implications for practice and is something that program faculty and co-op staff alike need to bear in mind when planning co-op experiences.

Fourth, a co-op work term learning plan, the opportunity to use previous learning, and a supportive co-op environment are important for students to be able to transfer their learning from the classroom to the cooperative education workplace experience. A co-op workplace environment that provides opportunities to use the knowledge and skills learned in the classroom is an important enabling factor to transfer these to the co-op workplace. The supportive involvement of the employer supervisor in the cooperative education experience, as reflected in participant comments in the cooperative education documentation and interview transcripts, is also important to support transfer of learning.

> My supervisor, you could bounce ideas off her left, right and center which was great when it came to the contracting side of things to be done . . . It was a very positive environment. You could wander anywhere and ask anyone anything, which was a real bonus.

Fifth, perceived barriers to transfer of learning also provide the opportunity for learning experiences. Although the barriers identified by the participants may have prevented them from transferring some of the learning in the program, they ultimately benefited from encountering these barriers. The specialized work experiences noted provided them with a focused learning experience, and dealing with organizational issues helped them to learn some valuable workplace-related skills. Co-op staff and employer supervisors can assist students to see the learning potential in difficult situations, especially recognizing that some barriers are not avoidable or able to be circumvented (Boud and Walker, 1993).

And finally, the program curriculum design plays a role in enabling the transfer of learning. The curriculum was designed with the expectation that students would transfer learning from the classroom to the co-op workplace. However, the academic course outlines for the first five of eight semesters appear to have been developed somewhat in isolation from the cooperative education experience and documentation with only an ad hoc connection being made between the two during academic courses. It would be interesting to see what difference more formal links between the academic courses and the co-op workplace learning experience would make. The findings show that the work term learning plan, a major component of the co-op documentation, is an effective tool to set the stage for the transfer of learning from the classroom to the cooperative education workplace. Encouraging the students to use the CLOs from their courses in the work term learning plan would be one way to foster this connection between the classroom curriculum and the co-op experience.

Recommendations for Practice

The findings of this research provide insight into what and how much learning is in fact transferred from the classroom to the cooperative education workplace. From the analysis of these findings several recommendations are offered related to practice.

Recommendation 1: Reinforce the importance of communication and technical skills for success in the cooperative education workplace experience with students. The findings of this research point to the fact that while students use different discipline-related knowledge and skills depending on the co-op work term experience, the communication and technical concepts and skills are used by all students in every cooperative education workplace experience. The evidence that these skills are used in all co-op workplace experiences could have an influence on students' engagement levels in the communication- and technology-related courses.

Recommendation 2: Design the academic course curriculum to link classroom learning with the cooperative education workplace experience to enable the students to transfer this learning more effectively. The cooperative education CLOs in this program establish the expectation that students are to transfer learning from the classroom to the cooperative education workplace experience, and the findings demonstrate that this occurs. However, this intentional link between the two learning environments is not obvious in the course outlines for the first five academic semesters. This is consistent with Milley's (2004) findings that when students returned to campus from co-op, the integration of their learning from work occurred in an ad hoc fashion (p. 272). In his study, as in this one, it was shown that professors played important informal roles in encouraging this integration of learning through their approaches to teaching. Case studies can take the place of a real situation in order to learn, especially if guidance is provided and if done in a supportive group environment (Van Gyn, 1996). Group discussions allow for feedback, questioning, exploration, clarification, and critique of ideas and skills. These not only stimulate exploration of new knowledge by the learners, but provide the opportunity for critical evaluation of the ideas presented in class (Nolan, 1994). Involvement of the faculty in the co-op planning process may also have an impact. By presenting students with the opportunity to use knowledge and skills during their academic courses within the frame of reference that they are preparing for their cooperative education workplace experiences and ultimately their future careers, they may be more able to see the connection between their classroom learning and the workplace, thus helping to break down the two solitudes.

Recommendation 3: Select cooperative education workplace experiences for students carefully to ensure alignment between the students' knowledge and abilities and the opportunities available to transfer the knowledge and skills learned in the classroom to the co-op workplace experience. The enablers and barriers to transfer of learning revealed in this research point to the importance of careful selection of cooperative education workplace experiences and careful matching with students. Both the college and the employers have key roles to play in this process. Planning of co-op experiences by college faculty and staff members in dialogue with the employers bearing in mind the students' current knowledge and ability may lead to co-op work term positions that allow students to work to their capacity.

Recommendation 4: Provide formal orientation and training to cooperative education employer supervisors to help them to understand their role, the program curriculum, and the level of the student more clearly. The students finalize their work term learning plans with the employer supervisors, and the employer supervisors conduct the midterm and final evaluations for the students. To do this effectively, employer supervisors need to have a good understanding of the program curriculum and have the ability to support the student to write effective learning objectives. They also need to understand their role in the co-op experience in order to ensure that the student is provided with the guidance, support, and supervision necessary to transfer learning from the classroom effectively, build on this learning, and also make a positive contribution in the workplace. Formal orientation and training for employer supervisors, along with resource materials, could be very helpful in achieving this. Any initiatives developed in this direction will need to keep in mind that employers will be conscious of their time commitment—they will want whatever they participate in kept simple. Ongoing support to employers during the work term from the college is also important.

Recommendation 5: Align the guidelines for the work term learning plan with the curriculum for the program, and guide students to use the CLOs from the academic courses studied prior to the particular co-op work term experience as a tool in developing co-op work term learning plans, with the goal of greater use and reinforcement of higher level classroom learning. The analyses of the learning that the students included in their work term learning plans provide a clear indication that they plan to use learning from the classroom and that they do use it. Use of the work term learning plan should be continued and encouraged. Additional guidance in the development of the learning objectives in the work term learning plans would be beneficial for students. In particular, revising the work term learning plan template to more closely align with the academic part of the curriculum would help students, faculty members, and employers make a direct link between the curriculum and the co-op experience. Encouraging the students to use the CLOs and the associated embedded knowledge and skills from their courses in all semesters as a guide when developing their work term learning plans would foster this link. This recommendation places emphasis on planning for concrete experiences based on previous experience. Engaging employers in discussion about the CLOs in the program through this process will provide a real-time link between the program and the world of work.

Recommendation 6: Add a planning and assessment tool to the cooperative education workplace experience that allows the student to both plan for and identify the CLOs transferred to the co-op work term. Participants in this research study completed the researcher-developed course learning outcomes questionnaire. Both the participants and the students who participated in the pilot study indicated that this was a useful tool. They said that it gave them a comprehensive picture of the learning that they brought from the classroom to the cooperative education workplace. It could also be used in planning discussions with employer supervisors to give them a clear picture of what the students coming to them have learned in the classroom prior to the co-op work term. While the course learning outcomes questionnaire was useful, any subsequent development should condense it further by developing summary statements from several similar CLOs to reduce the number of CLOs to a more manageable level.

Conclusion

The findings of this study provide a focused view of the issue of transfer of learning from the classroom to the cooperative education workplace in general and explore the relationship that students' learning styles have with this transfer of learning. They demonstrate that learning is indeed transferred from the classroom to the cooperative education workplace. Transfer of learning appears to be more closely linked to the co-op workplace experience itself than to the student's learning style. This study also shows the important role that curriculum design plays in facilitating the transfer of learning from the classroom to the co-op workplace. The findings of this research provide information that may be considered by those involved in developing and delivering cooperative education programs.

References

Apostolides, V., and Looye, J. W. "Developing Co-op Syllabi Sensitive for Both Academic Curricula and Employer Needs." *Journal of Cooperative Education*, 1997, 32(3), 56–69.

Beckett, D., and Hager, P. "Making Judgments as the Basis for Workplace Learning: Towards an Epistemology of Practice." *International Journal of Lifelong Education*, 2000, 19(4), 300–311.

Boud, D., Cohen, R., and Walker, D. "Introduction: Understanding Learning from Experience." In D. Boud, R. Cohen, and D. Walker (eds.), *Using Experience for Learning*, 1–17. Philadelphia: Open University Press, 1993.

Boud, D., and Walker, D. "Barriers to Reflection on Experience." In D. Boud, R. Cohen, and D. Walker (eds.), *Using Experience for Learning*, 73–86. Philadelphia: Open University Press, 1993.

Brew, A. "Unlearning through Experience." In D. Boud, R. Cohen, and D. Walker (eds.), *Using Experience for Learning*, 87–98. Philadelphia: Open University Press, 1993.

Canadian Council on Learning. The Benefits of Experiential Learning. Lessons in Learning Report, 2008, at www.ccl-cca.ca/CCL/Reports/LessonsInLearning

Chapman, A. Kolb Learning Styles. Businessballs.comWeb site, 2006, at www.businessballs.com/kolblearningstyles.htm

Cheek, G. D., and Campbell, C. "Help Them Use What They Learn." *Adult Learning*, 1994, 5(4), 27–28.

Davidge-Johnston, N. L. "The Nature of Learning in Cooperative Education in the Applied Sciences." Unpublished master's thesis, Faculty of Education, Simon Fraser University, Burnaby, B.C., Canada, 1996.

Donohue, M. M. "Transfer of Learning from the Classroom to the Cooperative Education Workplace in a Baccalaureate Program in an Ontario College of Applied Arts and

Technology." Unpublished doctoral dissertation, Department of Theory and Policy Studies, University of Toronto, Toronto, ON., Canada, 2010, at http://hdl.handle.net/1807/26169

Eakins, P. "The Importance of Context in Work Placements." *Journal of Cooperative Education*, 2000, 35(2–3), 61–67.

Eames, C. "Learning in the Workplace through Co-operative Education Placements: Beginning a Longitudinal Qualitative Study." *Journal of Cooperative Education*, 2000, 35(2/3), 76–83.

Flick, U. "Triangulation Revisited: Strategy of Validation or Alternative?" *Journal for the Theory of Social Behaviour*, 1992, 22(2), 175–197.

Grosjean, G. "Doing Co-op: Student Perceptions of Learning and Work." Unpublished doctoral dissertation, Department of Educational Studies, University of British Columbia, Vancouver, B.C., Canada, 2000.

Howard, A., and England-Kennedy, E. S. "Transgressing Boundaries through Learning Communities." *Journal of Cooperative Education*, 2001, 36(1), 76–82.

Johnson, R. B. "Examining the Validity Structure of Qualitative Research." *Education*, 1997, 118(2), 282–292.

Johnston, N., Angerilli, N., and Gajdamaschko, N. "How to Measure Complex Learning Processes: The Nature of Learning in Cooperative Education." In P. L. Linn, A. Howard, and E. Miller (eds.), *Handbook for Research in Cooperative Education and Internships*, 157–190. Mahwah, N.J.: Lawrence Erlbaum Associates, 2004.

Kolb, A. Y., and Kolb, D. A. "Learning Styles and Learning Spaces: Enhancing Experiential Learning in Higher Education." *Academy of Management Learning & Education*, 2005, 4(2), 193–212.

Kolb, D. A. *Experiential Learning: Experience as the Source of Learning and Development*. Englewood Cliffs, N.J.: Prentice-Hall, 1984.

Kolb, D. A. *Kolb Learning Style Inventory: Version 3.1*. Boston: Hay Resources Direct, 2005.

Loo, R. "A Meta-Analytic Examination of Kolb's Learning Style Preferences among Business Majors." *Journal of Education for Business*, 2002, 77(2), 252–256.

Milley, P. *The Social and Educational Implications of University Cooperative Education: A Habermasian Perspective*. Unpublished doctoral dissertation, Department of Educational Psychology and Leadership Studies, University of Victoria, Victoria, B.C., Canada, 2004.

Milne, P. "A Model for Work Integrated Learning: Optimizing Student Learning Outcomes." Paper presented at the World Association for Cooperative Education 6th Annual International Conference, Singapore, 2007.

Nolan, R. E. "From the Classroom to the Real World." *Adult Learning*, 1994, 5(4), 26.

Raschick, M., Maypole, D. E., and Day, P. A. "Improving Field Education through Kolb Learning Theory." *Journal of Social Work Education*, 1998, 34(1), 31–42.

Ricks, F., Van Gyn, G., Branton, G., Cutt, J., Loken, M., and Ney, T. "Theory and Research in Cooperative Education: Practice Implications." *Journal of Cooperative Education*, 1990, 27(1), 7–20.

Ryder, K. G. "Social and Educational Roots." In K. G. Ryder and J. W. Wilson (eds.), *Cooperative Education in a New Era: Understanding and Strengthening the Links between College and the Workplace*, 1–12. San Francisco: Jossey-Bass, 1987.

Saltmarsh, J. A. "John Dewey and the Future of Cooperative Education." *Journal of Cooperative Education*, 1992, 28(1), 6–16.

Skolnik, M. L. "The Community College Baccalaureate in Canada: Its Meaning and Implications for the Organization of Postsecondary Education, the Mission and Character of the Community College, and the Bachelor's Degree." Prepared for the First Annual Community College Baccalaureate Association Conference: Learning from the Past, Shaping the Future, Orlando, Florida, February 7–9, 2001, at http://cclp.mior.ca/Reference%20Shelf/Skolnik%20Paper%20Two.pdf

Stark, J. "The 'Iceberg Effect': Potential for Deeper Learning through Cooperative Education." Unpublished master's thesis, Department of Leadership Training, Royal Roads University, Victoria, B.C., Canada, 2004.

Van Gyn, G. H. "Reflective Practice: The Needs of Professions and the Promise of Cooperative Education." *Journal of Cooperative Education*, 1996, *31*(2), 103–131.

Vince, R. "Behind and Beyond Kolb's Learning Cycle." *Journal of Management Education*, 1998, 22(3), 304–319.

Weisz, M., and Kimber, D. "Ethics, Education, and Work: Reflections on Cooperative Education in the New University System." *Journal of Cooperative Education*, 2001, 36(2), 43–50.

MARGUERITE M. DONOHUE is Vice President of Academics at Canadore College in North Bay, Ontario, Canada.

MICHAEL L. SKOLNIK is Professor Emeritus of theory and policy studies in education at the University of Toronto, where he formerly held the William G. Davis Chair in Community College Leadership.

7

Mindful that applied baccalaureate degrees often have as their target audience adults who consider themselves workers first and students second, this chapter defines the AB degree, offers insights into why they are important, and presents results of a state-by-state inventory highlighting applied baccalaureate degree programs in Oklahoma and Washington.

Why Applied Baccalaureates Appeal to Working Adults: From National Results to Promising Practices

Debra Bragg, Collin Ruud

Largely overlooked in the past, working adults are increasingly recognized as a group that is underrepresented in higher education. Many adults seek the opportunity to enroll in college but struggle to find programs that accommodate their busy lives and their non-traditional participation. The National Center for Education Statistics (NCES) reports that students age twenty-five and older make up approximately 43 percent (fourteen million) of the students in U.S. higher education and further projects that these numbers will increase (2009). King (2006) estimates from 78 to 82 percent of nontraditional-age individuals work while attending college, with many viewing themselves as employees first and students second. Many adults entering college today are impacted by the nation's struggling economy, with substantial numbers being displaced or unemployed. Community colleges have been at the forefront of this problem, enrolling large numbers of students who need to re-enter the labor force (Mullin and Phillippe, 2009). Landing a job is top priority for these adults, but advancing in a career is important too.

Adults represent a student population that can benefit from new policies that emphasize college completion and credentialing, such as the American Graduation Initiative announced in 2009 by President Obama (Obama, 2009). The 2008 American Community Survey of the Census Bureau estimates that more than thirty-seven million adults have

New Directions for Community Colleges, no. 158, Summer 2012 © 2012 Wiley Periodicals, Inc.
Published online in Wiley Online Library (wileyonlinelibrary.com) • DOI: 10.1002/cc.20018

accumulated some college credits but no degrees (Lumina Foundation for Education, 2010). Adults who have participated in college without receiving credentials often seek to return to college for training to maintain their current jobs or to secure employment in new fields. Many colleges and universities have expanded adult enrollments, in part to respond to the nation's economic and unemployment crisis.

Recent economic changes have "put a premium on an educated workforce" (Chao, DeRocco, and Flynn, 2007, p. 3), reinforcing the importance of closer linkages between higher education and the education of adult workers. Carnevale, Smith, and Strohl (2010) claim postsecondary credentialing is critical, with 60 percent of jobs requiring a postsecondary credential of some sort by 2018. Adult learners are "a diverse and complex set of individuals with widely divergent aspirations, levels of preparation and degrees of risk" (Pusser et al., 2007, p. 2). They value the opportunity to build upon past experience to improve future career prospects. As a result, many seek applied technical education, including certificate and applied associate degrees that prepare students for immediate employment rather than transfer to a university. Townsend (2002) and others have observed that applied associate degrees prepare students for immediate employment with positive economic payoffs relative to a high school diploma or some college. However, this advantage is countered when these "terminal" degrees leave students with few options to pursue a baccalaureate education. Students having applied associate degrees may be denied admission by four-year universities or be admitted but experience course-by-course transcript audits that result in few credits applying to the bachelor's degree (Ruud and Bragg, 2011).

Recognizing the challenges adult learners experience, the Council for Adult and Experiential Learning (CAEL) (2008) noted that the most successful programs for adult learners anticipate the challenges these students face and build in program elements to address them. They recognize that adults need to integrate learning with other aspects of their lives (such as personal, family, work, community), and they employ alternative instructional delivery models, including online, and support services that can be accessed anytime and anywhere.

Looking beyond institutional strategies, the National Commission on Adult Literacy (2008) called for legislation that would make workforce preparation the primary goal of adult education, including addressing education for unemployed and lower-skilled workers, and other adult groups historically underserved by higher education. Further, state higher education boards are encouraging institutions to support increased adult enrollment (see, for example, Illinois Board of Higher Education, 2009), and federal policymakers and philanthropic organizations like Lumina Foundation for Education are promoting policies that award credentials to adults who return to college with some credit. Understanding the ways higher education can further support adult learners is a priority among all of these groups, and one of several reasons for the bright spotlight on applied baccalaureate degrees.

Applied Baccalaureate Degrees

Our multiphase research on applied baccalaureate (AB) degrees began in 2007 with an exclusive focus on public higher education institutions in all fifty states. The initial national inventory was completed in 2008 (Townsend, Bragg, and Ruud, 2008) and updated in summer 2010 (Bragg and Ruud, 2011; Ruud and Bragg, 2011). In the original inventory, data were collected using interviews of senior-level administrators of state agencies responsible for higher education and community college education through library and Web searches and through ongoing and extensive literature review. Following the creation of state profiles, state administrators and policy elites, including an advisory committee comprised of national experts, challenged our assumptions, advised on the accuracy and adequacy of our initial results, and strengthened the research process. In summer 2010, as part of conducting a policy meeting sponsored by the Lumina Foundation for Education, we reviewed the extant literature, major media outlets, and LexisNexis to identify states where new developments had occurred, and this information was used to update the national inventory.

Our results indicate that AB degree programs continue to evolve, including growth since 2007 when our research began and encompassing more states engaging in formal deliberations about AB policy, with some states authorizing institutions to award these degrees. Moreover, while some states engaged in formal deliberations and decided to adopt AB policy, it is important to note that others have concluded that ABs are not an appropriate option at this time, focusing instead on improving transfer and articulation. These alternative strategies are pursued to build partnerships and encourage shared resources between community colleges and universities and avoid system-level reforms that authorize new baccalaureate degree programs.

Despite the uncertainty and added requirements of AB degrees, some states have decided to support these degrees, citing their responsiveness to working adult learners who seek bachelor's credentials in business management, engineering and technology careers, nursing and other healthcare careers, and education and training (see, for example, Floyd, 2006). Though it is not true of all fields, the paths to secure careers in many of these fields is through occupationally specific, applied associate degrees (i.e., associates of applied science or A.A.S. degrees) that have historically been considered terminal, meaning students exit to employment without accumulating any or only very modest credits that transfer to baccalaureate degrees. Also, partly because of the terminal nature of applied associate degrees, students have had limited opportunity for career advancement to levels that require the baccalaureate, and this is problematic when the

NEW DIRECTIONS FOR COMMUNITY COLLEGES • DOI: 10.1002/cc

workforce requires such credentials. For this reason, our study deliberately positioned the AB degree as a countermovement to the historic terminal associate degree by defining it as:

> . . . a bachelor's degree [that is] designed to incorporate applied associate courses and degrees once considered as "terminal" or non-baccalaureate level while providing students with higher-order thinking skills and advanced technical knowledge and skills . . . (Townsend, Bragg, and Ruud, 2008).

In other words, these degrees take historically terminal applied associate degrees and coursework and allow most or all credits associated with them to transfer into baccalaureate-level degree programs, while also supplying the requisite general education and upper-division coursework necessary for a quality baccalaureate degree. This view of the AB is consistent with the prior work of numerous scholars who first defined the AB degree, particularly Ignash and Kotun (2005). This vision of the AB degree is not limited to a particular institution type, either community college or university. Rather, it suggests the AB is a type of baccalaureate degree separate and apart from institution type. It can be offered by a single two- or four-year institution, or it can involve transfer (upward and reverse) between institutions where articulation agreements are struck and resources are shared.

Moreover, our definition of the AB degree recognizes that all baccalaureate degrees require higher-order thinking skills that exceed those acquired at the associate level. Therefore, the AB degree is not simply about adding more college credits to an associate degree, but about increasing mastery of knowledge, skills, and dispositions commensurate with study at the upper division of the baccalaureate. This requirement recognizes that for the AB degree to be credible and lasting, it must be comparable in rigor and quality to other forms of baccalaureate degrees, such as the bachelor of arts (B.A.) and bachelor of science (B.S.).

State-by-State Inventory

The initial state-by-state inventory begun in 2007 found that thirty-nine of the fifty states had at least one four-year public institution offering an AB degree. According to state officials, ten of those thirty-nine states also had at least one traditional associate degree–granting institution—a community college, technical college, or two-year university branch campus with the authority to grant an AB degree according to our definition. Figure 7.1 provides a graphic depiction of the fifty states as of summer 2010 according to AB degree type, with states in light gray being those with traditional baccalaureate-degree granting institutions only and states in dark gray being those with traditional baccalaureate-degree granting institutions as well as traditional associate-degree granting institutions. States in medium gray

NEW DIRECTIONS FOR COMMUNITY COLLEGES • DOI: 10.1002/cc

Figure 7.1.   State-by-State Inventory, as of August 2010

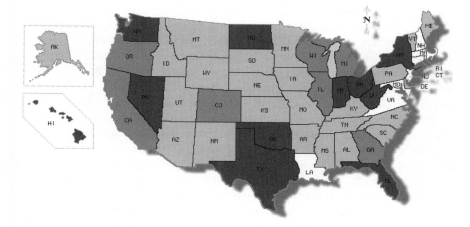

have current activity pertaining to the AB, including relatively new legislation or current debate in the legislative and administrative arenas.

Looking to the medium gray states, Colorado authorized one community college to plan baccalaureate degree programs to enhance geographic access for students located in remote mountain communities. States such as Michigan and California have proposed legislation, and debate remains active among policymakers. If approved, these states would allow for community college baccalaureates in a number of fields, including applied and technical fields. Oregon passed legislation that allowed for the state to examine the feasibility of implementing AB degrees. Michigan, California, and Illinois have all had legislation proposed or passed through at least one branch of the legislature that, if approved, would allow for community college baccalaureates in a number of fields, including applied majors. Georgia's higher education system has gone through significant redesign that may pave the way for changes to or growth in AB degrees. Finally, the University of Wisconsin System has approved the provision of bachelor of applied arts and sciences (B.A.A.S.) degrees at two-year branch campuses, although it is unclear whether these B.A.A.S. degrees would allow for the transfer of applied associate coursework or degrees.

Although there are more AB degrees offered by traditional baccalaureate degree–granting institutions, a great deal of attention has been paid to the awarding of AB degrees by traditionally associate-degree institutions, primarily community colleges, possibly due to the controversy that adoption of baccalaureate degrees represents for these institutions (Ruud and

Bragg, 2011). With respect to community college baccalaureate (CCB) degrees, our inventory focuses on current degrees, which distinguishes our results from others who report a higher number of states with baccalaureate-awarding two-year institutions. For example, Russell (2010) reported eighteen states with institutions awarding CCBs, most of which are AB degrees, but our 2010 inventory offers a more modest count that fairly closely matches Floyd and Walker (2009). Addressing the discrepancy in the number of states awarding CCBs in the literature, Floyd (2006) pointed out the Community College Baccalaureate Association (CCBA), a professional organization that serves institutions awarding the CCB, considers all community and technical colleges ever authorized to award baccalaureate degrees in its total count of CCB-awarding institutions no matter whether the institution later considers itself a primarily associate- or baccalaureate-awarding institution. In contrast, our count considers institutions as CCB-awarding if the state considers them as such, despite their classification by Carnegie or accreditation status. Therefore, because many states have associate degree-granting institutions now awarding baccalaureate degrees, and the officials in these states consider them predominantly baccalaureate degree-granting, our count is more conservative than other studies.

With regard to the CCB degree, several relevant discussions arose in conversations with state and institutional officials, as well as other events featuring dialogue on AB degrees. The first pertains to the issue of mission creep. Officials at two-year institutions that offer CCB degrees have widely asserted that, rather than reflect the definition of mission creep, the CCB, particularly in applied fields, recognizes changes in the labor market that make the transfer of applied associate degrees a logical extension to the baccalaureate. The workforce nature of AB degrees makes them fit well with the occupational-technical education mission of community and technical colleges. As more occupations require baccalaureate degrees for employment or advancement, traditional associate degree-granting college officials note they are meeting the demand of their students and employers by awarding these degrees.

CCB degrees are also seen as a means of offering more affordable post-secondary education for students of color, working adults, and low-income learners who find the tuition and fees of traditional baccalaureate-degree granting institutions out of reach. National experts have called for greater affordability in higher education, and policymakers have endorsed community colleges and other two-year institutions as institutions of choice to increase access as well as completion (Russell, 2010). From our research, it is also apparent that the CCB has emerged as a response in states where other solutions have not worked. For example, the CCB in Florida emerged in large part because the four-year institutions were unable to meet student demand in key workforce areas, particularly health care and teacher preparation. In Washington, legislation that created AB degrees at two-year institutions did so to increase the number of baccalaureate graduates within the state. In comparison to peer states, Washington, like Florida, is a high producer of associate degrees but a relatively low producer of baccalaureate graduates.

Applied Baccalaureate Models

Whether offered by a community college or university, extant literature suggests that AB degrees consist in different forms. As noted elsewhere in a volume by Ignash and Kotun (2005), different models of the AB degree exist as follows: "1) career ladder, 2) inverse or upside down, and 3) management ladder degrees" (p. 115). Like Ignash and Kotun, we found these three models to be prevalent among institutions documented in our inventory and subsequent case study research (Bragg and Ruud, 2011), along with newer hybrid approaches that borrow components to customize AB degree programs for diverse student populations. Science, technology, mathematics, and engineering (STEM) programs that use the hybrid model continue to be under investigation in our larger work on the AB, with funding from the National Science Foundation (NSF).

This section profiles two AB degrees, describing programs, policies, and instructional strategies that seek to meet the needs of working adults. The two programs featured in this chapter provide an example of the career ladder and management models in occupational and technical fields important to the local economy.

AB Degrees at Oklahoma State University Institute of Technology

The Oklahoma State University Institute of Technology (OSU-IT) is located in Okmulgee, approximately thirty-five miles south of Tulsa. Formerly known as Oklahoma State University–Okmulgee, the campus underwent a formal name change authorized by the state legislature in 2008. As of 2008–2009, OSU-IT enrolled 5,090 students (i.e., 3,027 FTE) and awarded 516 associate degrees and forty-three baccalaureate degrees. The core mission revolves around the preparation of a "diverse student body" through "comprehensive, high-quality, advancing technology programs and services" to be "competitive members of a world-class workforce and contributing members of society" (OSU Institute of Technology, n.d.). The institution awards associate of applied science (A.A.S.) degrees, with a few associate of science (A.S.) degrees in areas such as pre-education, business, and information technology.

About eight years ago, administrators began discussions to consider whether technical baccalaureate programs should be moved from the main campus of Oklahoma State University (OSU) to two-year technical branch campuses in the state. While the system decided not to move bachelor of technology (B.T.) degrees away from the four-year campuses of the OSU

NEW DIRECTIONS FOR COMMUNITY COLLEGES • DOI: 10.1002/cc

system, eventually the system began to allow the technical branches to award B.T. degrees in limited, technical fields.

OSU-IT presently offers B.T. degrees in information assurance and forensics, instrumentation engineering technology, and civil engineering technology. These degree fields were identified through OSU-IT's strong relationships with employers to address the regional demand for workers. In addition to hiring faculty with industry experience, a group of industry advisors consults with faculty and administrators on general education needs, courses that are (and are not) applicable to the workforce, and other employment-related issues. A high level of employer involvement is especially apparent in the twenty-nine-member advisory committee for the information technologies (IT) program, which is comprised mostly of upper-level managers from local companies and international corporations.

Administrators at OSU-IT acknowledge that all three B.T. degrees most closely resemble the career ladder model, as the programs are technically specialized, requiring forty-four and fifty-four credits of general education course work, per state requirements, that are also carefully integrated with technical content. For example, a professor of technical content noted that a calculus professor seeks occupational subject matter to integrate into curriculum and enrich instruction. He observed that the calculus professor "actually comes over, sits with our faculty, and says 'Give me some examples of how I can put [what you're teaching] in my curriculum so there's a tie there'."

Beyond the forty-four to fifty-four general education credit requirement, most, if not all, of the remaining coursework is directly applicable to the technical field of the BT degree. The applied nature of the BT degree is best exemplified in the information assurance and forensics BT degree requirement of thirty-three credits of 1000/2000 (freshman/sophomore) level courses in information technologies and information assurance and forensics; thirty-seven credit hours of 3000/4000 level courses, fifty-three credit hours of general education, and a one-credit cornerstone (introduction/orientation) course, for a total of 124 credit hours. Courses are offered in a variety of settings and at a range of times to accommodate the diversity of students who enroll in the programs, including working adults and students who need to enroll part-time. To accommodate their need to fit school with busy work lives, many classes have sections that meet on nights and weekends only, and some courses are offered entirely online or in a hybrid online/on-campus format. One faculty member explained, we're doing a lot online, but we've also investigated a hybrid, where the theory side is all online and then [students] come to campus for the technical side of it. So instead of being here five days a week, they're maybe only here one evening and a Saturday.

This recommendation came about specifically to address the needs of nontraditional learners who requested more online options. Faculty members see the hybrid approach as a feasible approach to deliver the technical content in their B.T. degrees, since the applied nature of the content requires hands-on learning. They also acknowledge that new technologies, including virtual environments, may make it possible to mimic hands-on learning in online environments.

The B.T. degrees offered by OSU-IT are all within fields where the campus also offers a corresponding A.A.S. degree. As a result, many B.T. students enter as freshmen intending to complete the B.T. degree at the associate level, but decide to continue to a baccalaureate. As a policy, students are not technically part of the B.T. program until their third year, where they must "re-apply" and go through additional requirements, such as a personal background check for students who seek admission to the information assurance and forensics program. However, the language used in the program's catalog states that "The Bachelor of Technology programs are designed so that a student will earn a corresponding associate degree during his or her pursuit of the BT degree" (*OSU Institute of Technology Catalog*, 2009). The offering of an AB degree in such a "standalone" form is not common among the institutions we visited as part of our national study, but it represents one way in which institutions that have historically awarded mostly or solely associate degrees are creating new pathways to the baccalaureate.

AB Degrees at South Seattle Community College

South Seattle Community College (SSCC) is one of three community colleges (i.e., South, Central, and North) that make up the Seattle Community College District serve which/s the metropolitan Seattle area. The district is easily the largest in the state, serving nearly 55,000 students annually, and one of the largest and most highly diverse higher education institutions in the northwest United States. The district's comprehensive mission, which includes a sizeable curriculum focused on professional and technical education, is credited with helping the Seattle area move from a predominantly manufacturing economy to a more diversified, particularly information-based economy (Seattle Community Colleges, n.d.).

SSCC's foray into the AB is tied to Washington's passage of House Bill 1794 to create pilot AB degree programs in four community colleges (Ruud, Bragg, and Townsend, 2010). Beginning in 2005, the legislation authorized the piloting of AB degree programs at the two- and four-year levels, with AB degree programs awarded by community and technical colleges and with branch campuses expanding their mission by offering lower-division courses and supporting more flexibility in the admission of transfer students. An important goal of the legislation was to expand baccalaureate attainment by approving AB degree programs at institutions besides the University of Washington and Washington State University, where nearly 50 percent of baccalaureate degrees were being awarded at the time (Ignash,

2010). With the capacity for awarding baccalaureate degrees fully tapped at these institutions, the state needed alternative approaches to fulfill its goal of increasing baccalaureate attainment statewide.

The Higher Education Coordinating Board (HECB) strategic plan claimed nearly 40,000 citizens should be encouraged to pursue additional education (Ignash, 2010: Ruud, Bragg, and Townsend, 2010), calling for redesign of the state's higher education delivery system to include a new process for determining when and where to build new campuses and centers, develop new programs, and expand eLearning and other delivery modes. The plan called for these changes within a 10-year framework between 2008 and 2018, but the severity of the recession has extended implementation of some aspects of the plan for more than a decade. Front and center in these recommendations is the expansion of AB degree programs.

The HECB positioned AB degrees as pathways for applied associate degree graduates, using the associate of applied science-transfer (A.A.S.-T.) degree as the vehicle for recognizing lower-division credits toward the baccalaureate. First approved in 2002, the A.A.S.-T. requires that a minimum of twenty credits of general education courses drawn from the direct transfer agreement be accepted toward the baccalaureate, recognizing that these courses serve a dual purpose of employment as well as transfer. AB degrees in Washington typically culminate in the B.A.S., but they can also matriculate to a B.A. or B.S.

As part of the initial pilot, South Seattle Community College (SSCC) made the decision to develop and award an AB degree in hospitality management to students who completed the A.A.S.-T. degree in accounting, business information technology, culinary, or other related programs. Information on the SSCC Web site notes that the degree is designed to remove roadblocks that prevent students who hold the A.A.S.-T. degree from using credits toward their baccalaureate, and program faculty and students acknowledge the importance of recognizing credits in the A.A.S.-T. package. Other goals that pertain to the importance of this AB degree program include the importance of attracting qualified working adults; recruiting and preparing diverse students, including students of color, English language learners, and first-generation students, for the local hospitality industry; and contributing to state and regional economic goals.

Students enrolled in the hospitality management program, which is representative of the management model, learn about supervision, management, marketing, and human resources in the context of the hospitality industry, including tourism, hotel operations, restaurant management, catering, cruise ship operations, casino operations, and travel. The program also serves rapidly expanding industry sectors, such as assisted and independent living facilities in the Puget Sound region, which has an increasing population of retirees and elderly citizens. The hospitality management degree, the only one of its kind on the west side of Washington, is purported to address significant unmet industry demand for skilled and diverse workers in the Seattle-King County metropolitan area and in Washington state, contributing to regional and state economic development goals.

Beside classroom instruction, the program requires a thousand-hour internship, which is linked to a high success (i.e., completion and placement) rate: In 2009–2010, 93 percent of the graduates continued to work or took new jobs in the hospitality industry. An ESL learner who described himself as "a hands-on guy" and was reaching the end of the program summarized his success by saying,

> I chose to go to a community college first because I wasn't sure what I wanted to do. [I]t was a good place to get my feelers out and take classes and see what I enjoyed. I was happy when they set this [AB degree] program up because it made it easy for me to get my bachelor. It's a great program to be in.

Reflecting a perspective shared by many hospitality management students, this learner was grateful to be able to pursue a baccalaureate degree that he felt confident would translate into future career opportunities.

Conclusion: Promising Practices

Applied baccalaureate degree programs use various models (e.g., career ladder, inverted, management, and hybrid) that facilitate the enrollment of working adults and accommodate the demands of students, who have complex, multifaceted lives. Linking coursework focused on academic and technical competencies to prior work experience and finding ways to extend students' learning about related careers with growth opportunities are important goals. Combining these strategies with evening and weekend scheduling, online instruction, capstone courses, internships, and credit for life/work experience is evident in many AB programs. Services that support student enrollment and retention to ensure that the baccalaureate degree is a viable option and that entry into and advancement in employment is an achievable goal are important to students and a necessity for successful AB degree programs.

Recognized by some states as an important development, we believe AB degrees are a potentially important ingredient in the nation's formula to increase baccalaureate completion. The degrees do not need to be tied exclusively to a particular institution type, although the possibility that they can be offered by traditional associate degree-granting institutions in addition to baccalaureate degree-granting institutions makes them easier to scale up to reach more learners. AB degree programs that offer a career pathway enabling working adults who are underserved by higher education to advance from the applied associate to the baccalaureate degree are an important breakthrough. Increasing access and further diversifying baccalaureate degree attainment is an important goal for nearly every state. In achieving this objective, the states will undoubtedly address another key goal, which is to prepare a more highly skilled workforce.

References

Bragg, D. D., & Ruud, C. M. *The Adult Learner and the Applied Baccalaureate: Lessons from Six States.* Champaign, IL.: Office of Community College Research and Leadership, May 2011.

Carnevale, A. P., Smith, N., & Strohl, J. Help Wanted: Projections of Jobs and Education Requirements through 2018. Washington D.C.: Georgetown University, Center on Education and the Workforce, June 2010, at http://www9.georgetown.edu/grad/gppi/hpi/cew/pdfs/FullReport.pdf

Chao, E. L., DeRocco, E. S., & Flynn, M. K. Adult learners in higher education: Barriers to success and strategies to improve results. Washington, D.C.: Employment and Training Administration, March 2007, at http://wdr.doleta.gov/research/FullText_Documents/Adult%20Learners%20in%20Higher%20Education%20-%20Barriers%20to%20Success%20and%20Strategies%20to%20Improve%20Results.pdf

Council for Adult and Experiential Learning. Adult Learning in Focus: National and State-by-State Data. Chicago, Ill.: Author, 2008, at http://www.cael.org/pdfs/State_Indicators_Monograph

Floyd, D. L. "Achieving the Baccalaureate through the Community College." In D. D. Bragg and E. A. Barnett (eds.), *Special Issue: Academic Pathways to and from the Community College.* New Directions for Community Colleges, no. 135. San Francisco: Jossey-Bass, 2006.

Floyd, D. L., and Walker, K. "The Community College Baccalaureate: Putting the Pieces Together." *Community College Journal of Research and Practice*, 2009, 33(2), 90–124.

Ignash, J. "System Design: Washington's Plan to Guide Expansion of the State's Higher Education System." Paper presentation for the Council for the Study of Community Colleges in Seattle, WA., April 16, 2010.

Ignash, J., and Kotun, D. "Results of a National Study of Transfer in Occupational/Technical Degrees: Policies and Practices." *Journal of Applied Research in the Community College*, 2005, 12(2), 109–120.

Illinois Board of Higher Education. "The Illinois Public Agenda for College and Career Success." Springfield, Ill.: Author, June 2009, at www.ibhe.state.il.us/masterPlanning/materials/070109_PublicAgenda.pdf

King, J. "Working Their Way Through College: Student Employment and Its Impact on the College Experience." Washington, D.C.: American Council on Education, May 2006, at www.acenet.edu/AM/Template.cfm?template=/CM/ContentDisplay.cfm&ContentFileID=1618

Lumina Foundation for Education. A Stronger Nation through Higher Education. Indianapolis, Ind.: Author, 2010, at www.luminafoundation.org/publications/A_stronger_nation.pdf

Mullin, C., & Phillippe, K. (2009). "Community College Enrollment Surge: An Analysis of Estimated Fall 2009 Headcount Enrollment." Washington, D.C.: American Association of Community Colleges, December 2009, at www.aacc.nche.edu/newsevents/News/articles/Documents/ccenrollmentsurge2009.pdf

National Center for Education Statistics. *Digest of Education Statistics, 2008* (NCES 2009–020). Washington, D.C.: Author, 2009.

National Commission on Adult Literacy. "Reach Higher, America: Overcoming Crisis in the U.S. Workforce." A Report of the National Commission on Adult Literacy, June 2008, at www.nationalcommissiononadultliteracy.org/ReachHigherAmerica/ReachHigher.pdf

Obama, B. "The American Graduation Initiative." The White House, Office of the Press Secretary. Washington, D.C., 2009.

OSU Institute of Technology. OSU Institute of Technology Catalog. OSU Institute of Technology Web site, 2009, at www.osuit.edu/academics/forms/catalog_2009.pdf

OSU Institute of Technology. Mission. OSU Institute of Technology Web site, n.d., at www.osuit.edu/campus_community/mission.html

Pusser, B., Breneman, D. W., Gansneder, B. M., Kohl, K. J., Levin, J. S., Milam, J. H., and Turner, S. E. "Returning to Learning: Adults' Success in College Is Key to America's Future." Indianapolis, Ind.: Lumina Foundation for Education, March 2007, at www.luminafoundation.org/publications/ReturntolearningApril2007.pdf

Russell, A. "Update on the Community College Baccalaureate: Evolving Trends and Issues." Policy Matters: A Higher Education Policy Brief, American Association of State Colleges and Universities, Washington, DC, October 2010, at http://www.aascu.org/uploadedFiles/AASCU/Content/Root/PolicyAndAdvocacy/PolicyPublications/AASCU_Update_Community_College_Baccalaureate(1).pdf

Ruud, C., and Bragg, D. "The Applied Baccalaureate: What We Know, What We Learned, and What We Need to Know." Champaign, Ill.: Office of Community College Research and Leadership, University of Illinois, 2011, at http://occrl.illinois.edu/files/Projects/lumina/Paper/AB_Convening_Paper.pdf

Ruud, C. M., Bragg, D. D., and Townsend, B. K. "The Applied Baccalaureate Degree: The Right Time and Place." Community College Journal of Research and Practice, 2010, 34(1), 136–152.

Seattle Community Colleges. College History. Seattle Community Colleges Web site, n.d., at www.seattlecolleges.com/DISTRICT/district/history.aspx

Townsend, B. Transfer Students Do Transfer. Paper presentation at the American Association of Community Colleges Conference in Seattle, WA., 2002. (ED 464 696).

Townsend, B., Bragg, D., and Ruud, C. "The Adult Learner and the Applied Baccalaureate: National and State-by-State Inventory." Columbia, MO.: Center for Community College Research, University of Missouri-Columbia, 2008.

DEBRA BRAGG is a professor of education policy, organization and leadership at the University of Illinois at Urbana-Champaign.

COLLIN RUUD is a doctoral student of education policy, organization and leadership at the University of Illinois at Urbana-Champaign.

NEW DIRECTIONS FOR COMMUNITY COLLEGES • DOI: 10.1002/cc

8

This chapter identifies some of the challenges facing the applied and workforce baccalaureate. The authors seek not to argue against the baccalaureate but rather to identify concerns that need to be addressed in order to design and implement the degree effectively.

Institutional Challenges of Applied and Workforce Baccalaureate Programs

Richard L. Wagoner, Carlos Ayon

The editors and authors of this volume have clearly documented that the community college baccalaureate degree movement has gained momentum during the past decade, especially the applied and workforce baccalaureate. Proponents of these models believe they provide the access and capacity necessary to supply local economies with skilled workers in business and industry sectors such as allied health, technology, education, and mid-level management. Additionally, they cite community colleges' philosophy to serve their immediate community needs as further evidence of the necessity of community colleges to provide baccalaureate degrees. But what of the critics of community college baccalaureate models who argue that the already stretched mission and operations of community colleges will suffer as institutions increase offerings and expand programs? These individuals also suggest the potential that community colleges will cease to exist as 2-year institutions with traditional missions, as they move toward a 4-year college model (Eaton, 2005; Levin, 2004; Wattenbarger, 2000). Beyond these concerns regarding community college mission and institutional identity, there are also concerns about community college faculty with respect to their required qualifications and the work they are expected to perform.

We do not suggest in this chapter that the community college applied baccalaureate should be eliminated, or even curtailed. We do believe, however, that it is important to discuss potential challenges regarding mission,

NEW DIRECTIONS FOR COMMUNITY COLLEGES, no. 158, Summer 2012 © 2012 Wiley Periodicals, Inc.
Published online in Wiley Online Library (wileyonlinelibrary.com) • DOI: 10.1002/cc.20019

institutional identity, and faculty for college leaders, practitioners, and policy makers to address when seeking to create or maintain AWBs. Our discussion in this chapter is based on the review of ideas that have already been documented in both the scholarly and practical literature, and it offers an illustration of those points with current developments and our perspectives about this degree.

The Challenge to the Community College Mission

For over a decade practitioners and scholars have questioned whether community college baccalaureates will stretch the already numerous missions of modern comprehensive community colleges (Eaton, 2005; Levin, 2004; Wattenbarger, 2000). In what is certainly the most thorough and detailed exploration of this possibility, Levin (2004) argues that much of the impetus to broaden the community college mission through the baccalaureate is a product of the global economy and the market expansion it seems to demand. This argument is drawn in careful detail and, while we cannot review it in full here, we advise anyone interested in this topic to closely read this work. However, we do have two particular points we would like to emphasize along this line.

First, as Levin argues, when a global economic rationale is employed, "markets, not citizens" (2004, p. 3) become the focus of institutions. This certainly would be a situation antithetical to the traditionally understood mission of colleges to serve local citizens. While we don't believe this in itself is negative, we agree with Levin that it certainly adds an additional level of mission that poses an interesting conundrum for college leaders, practitioners, and policy makers seeking to create or maintain AWBs. Second, we point to the language and rationale of several of the chapters in this volume which cite preparing workers and their local regions and states as one of the major motivations to pursue AWBs. Again, we do not judge this position; we only use this as an example that furthers the arguments articulated by Levin (2004). Those concerns have not disappeared in the past eight years; they exist still.

Similar questions from a less theoretical perspective have also come from other published higher education literature. Townsend (2005), regarding community colleges offering the baccalaureate, raised concerns over the future of the community college as an institutional type and the redirection of resources away from the traditional missions of community colleges. Wattenbarger (2000) argued strongly that community college baccalaureates will stretch the limited resources of colleges and potentially cause them to produce what might be considered second-rate degrees. He also maintained that colleges could function more effectively as an intermediary for their students as a means for offering various pathways to the baccalaureate—the theme of *New Directions for Community Colleges* volume 135. Eaton (2005) argued a similar point, emphasizing the community colleges' long-standing role as a major point of access for students to begin college level studies. For both authors, community colleges are able to do what they do best because they focus on the first two years of post-secondary education, giving them the means to maximize the use of their limited resources. Offering baccalaureate degrees, then, would force colleges to embrace new missions and programs, which in turn has the potential to create "new regulations, norms, and cognitive systems" (Levin, 2004, p. 15).

We have seen evidence of this in our field research. This type of institutional behavior was witnessed at a Canadian college that was in the process of transforming into a baccalaureate institution (Levin, 2004; Levin, Kater, & Wagoner, 2006). At the time of the fieldwork, the college had not yet become a baccalaureate institution, but academic leaders at all levels discussed decisions about curriculum, program maintenance and development, and hiring based on models reflecting a baccalaureate institution as opposed to the current two-year models and expectations. The policies and practices anticipated the transformation of the institution. The college's mission was not merely expanding, but the coming change was receiving an ever-increasing share of resources, while programs aside from the baccalaureate received fewer resources and found their place at the college threatened.

Baccalaureate programs undoubtedly create new policies, practices, and systems; the chapters in this volume illuminate that very point. Even when a college builds upon a successful non-baccalaureate program, it must by necessity create new policies and practices to accommodate the expanded program. Of course this expansion process would be considerably more pronounced for a college developing an AWB program from the ground up. Whether an AWB is an expansion of an already-established program within a college or an entirely new one, it will need increased resources, both human and capital, to develop and thrive. Given the relative scarcity of resources colleges have been experiencing over the past several years in the aftermath of the great recession, we put forward that the new and increased resources of the AWB programs in some instances must come at the expense of other programs at colleges. While this type of resource re-allocation has certainly always occurred at community colleges, taking resources from two-year programs and granting them to baccalaureate programs has the potential not only to increase the mission of colleges, but to change the overall identity of institutions as well.

Threats to Community College Institutional Identity

Should a two-year institution be authorized to grant four-year degrees? This may be the most basic and perhaps essential question that has been addressed regarding the potential institutional challenges that AWBs pose. While we do acknowledge that the notion of using measures of time to describe educational programs completed based on credits earned continues to vex institutions, students, parents, and policy makers alike, the distinction still points to real differences between two- and four-year institutions. The authors in this volume answer this basic question with a "yes," even if they may at times qualify that positive response. In this section we would like to point to several instances where an affirmative answer to this essential question may not be so clear-cut.

There has been a general idea presented by authors who have questioned community college baccalaureates that asserts that if community colleges offer four-year degrees, they will cease to be community colleges (Eaton, 2005; Townsend, 2005; Wattenbarger, 2000). On the whole we believe that this volume helps to dispel that basic premise, but the waters do become troubled when we delve further into the question. Previous research has documented that numerous community colleges have taken on a changed or entirely new identity as the result of offering baccalaureate degrees. Levin (2004) analyzed examples from Canada and several U.S. states and concluded that baccalaureate programs bring changing student demographics, increased institutional autonomy, and university-style governance among other factors that, at the very least, indicate a new community college identity and perhaps even a new variant of a four-year college.

Regional accrediting bodies offer an additional insight into how this change in institutional identity can manifest itself. In a 2001 report, The Higher Learning Commission of the North Central Association of Colleges and Schools addressed the community college baccalaureate in a favorable manner, indicating that from an accreditation perspective it could be possible for community colleges to offer baccalaureate degrees. A closer reading of one of the commission's major recommendations, however, suggests the potential for a change in institutional identity. The task force's second recommendation states that accreditation of CCBs should "apply established criteria requirements and expectations for general education, institutional capacity, commitment of resources, and assessment of achieved student learning for the baccalaureate program" (p. 4). This language is somewhat vague, but if these areas must meet the requirements and expectations of other baccalaureate institutions (4-year colleges and universities), then it is not unreasonable to suggest that community colleges that received accreditation for baccalaureate programs would change their identities to fit the norms of other baccalaureate institutions accredited by the same body.

In the years since both the report cited above and Levin's (2004) analysis of institutional identity there have been several developments indicating that community college institutional identity has continued to change relative to the granting of baccalaureate degrees. The most recent and arguably most dramatic of these changes occurred in the state of Florida, where legislation (Florida Statutes, §1007.33, 2007) granted colleges the authorization to offer bachelor's degrees for the purpose of meeting the local workforce needs. As discussed in this volume, Florida has been at the forefront of recent innovation in CCBs, and while we do not submit that this sweeping change is the direct or sole result of AWBs being offered at community colleges in the state, it is undeniable that the road to this major shift in institutional identity was paved in part by the development of baccalaureate programs. The state of Utah has witnessed a similar pattern. As of 2012 the state now only has two two-year colleges—Salt Lake Community College and Snow College. Over the years, two former two-year schools, Weber State University and Utah Valley University, have moved to become designated as universities; one, Dixie State College, has become a four-year institution; and, most recently, one, Utah State University Eastern, has been merged with the state's land-grant university. In all of these cases the transformed institutions do still offer two-year degrees and programs, but their institutional identities have expanded beyond those of traditional two-year colleges.

In an article not specifically focused on CCBs, Brint (2003) illustrates how changing institutional identity can possibly change goals, programs, and even faculty. The author proposes that the ideal model for community colleges, however unlikely due to vested interests and costs among other factors, would be to separate into three distinct institutions: job training, baccalaureate pathway, and community education. In this hypothetical case, each of the three institutions would have very distinct programs and identities and would require very different faculties. While the former two-year colleges in Florida and Utah discussed above may not have entirely jettisoned all vestiges of lower-level training and community education, the designation of being four-year institutions certainly suggests changes in what is demanded of faculty.

The Role of Faculty

As community colleges come to develop and offer baccalaureate programs of any type, the role of faculty becomes a central issue. Traditionally faculty at community colleges are only required to hold a master's degree. This is in part due to the fact that colleges have only offered lower-level college courses. Also, community college faculty have no obligation to research or publish, and their service requirements have usually been limited to their home institution. Even if a community college develops a single applied baccalaureate, questions can arise about the faculty involved in that program. Obviously those questions will become more critical as the number of baccalaureates increases at an institution. Decisions will have to be made as to what the educational requirements will be for faculty. For instance, all faculty might be required to hold a terminal degree, or perhaps a terminal degree would be required to teach an upper-division class. It is possible that as more faculty are hired with terminal degrees there will be a greater emphasis toward research on the part of either the institution, the faculty, or both. Additionally, faculty who hold terminal degrees are acculturated to the view that part of their service should be to their academic field or specialty, moving their service focus away from being institution-centric. One potential outcome for a college that must distinguish between upper- and lower-division courses and those who are qualified to teach them is that terminal degrees may become the norm for instructors. Those with only master's degrees will be relegated to teaching solely lower-level courses with a resulting two-tier hierarchy among full-time faculty, increasing an already-disjointed faculty based on full- and part-time status and academic discipline (Levin, Kater, and Wagoner, 2006). Once terminal degrees are required, the overall role of faculty could certainly begin to morph into that of university faculty with research expectations and changing service roles, moving more from institutional service to service to state and national organizations.

At the same Canadian college discussed earlier where our field work has been conducted, many academic divisions hired only new faculty with terminal degrees for several years in anticipation of transforming to a baccalaureate institution (Levin, 2004; Levin, Kater, & Wagoner, 2006). At that institution, faculty had begun to expect the teaching loads and research support offered to university faculty, which from the faculty perspective was evidence of the type of changing institutional identity described by Levin (2004). To offer another example, faculty at Utah State University Eastern (formerly the College of Eastern Utah) have had some level of research added to their role statements. And while it has not yet become an official policy to hold a terminal degree, a number of faculty without such a credential have begun to make moves to acquire one. At the same time, many faculty have increased their activity related to national scholastic organizations and have begun serving those groups in addition to the local campus (Wagoner, 2011).

Conclusion

As we stated in our introduction, our intention in this chapter is not to condemn the AWB. We have, however, suggested that concerns voiced in previous literature are not merely "myths" (Floyd, 2006), but are real considerations about these programs that should not be dismissed. What we have attempted to do is provide some evidence (Wagoner, 2011) that the concerns of scholars and practitioners regarding AWBs have come to pass with respect to select cases in the United States and in Canada (Levin, 2004; Levin, Kater, & Wagoner, 2006). There is little doubt that institutional missions and their related finances have been stretched as AWBs have continued to develop, and particularly in times of budgetary trouble, these new missions might serve to displace other missions of the community college. Also, as witnessed in the cases of Florida, Utah, and Canada, institutional identity has been not only challenged, but transformed. While it may still be possible to have a baccalaureate institution fill the missions and programs of a community college, it is unclear if institutions will remain dedicated to those missions that do not add to institutional prestige. Finally, the role of faculty at colleges that offer baccalaureates do change and the expectations of them regarding minimum qualifications and work come to look more like university professors than traditional community college faculty who teach lower divisions courses and serve the college and its students almost exclusively. The challenges presented by community college applied baccalaureates should not be dismissed; they should be thoughtfully considered and frequently reviewed by scholars, practitioners, and policy makers as baccalaureate programs are developed, implemented, and as they mature.

References

Brint, S. "Few Remaining Dreams: Community Colleges Since 1985." *The Annals of the American Academy of Political and Social Science,* 2003, 586(1), 16–37.

Eaton, J. S. "Why Community Colleges Shouldn't Offer Baccalaureates." *Chronicle of Higher Education,* 2005, 52(10), B25.

Florida Statutes. §1007.33, 2007.

Floyd, D. "Achieving the Baccalaureate through the Community College." In D. D. Bragg and E. A. Barnett (eds.), *Special Issue: Academic Pathways to and from the Community College.* New Directions for Community Colleges, no. 135. San Francisco: Jossey-Bass, 2006.

Higher Learning Commission North Central Association of Colleges and Schools. "Baccalaureate Education in the Community College Setting. Task Force Executive Summary with Recommendations," 2001, at http://www.anacalifornia.org/cc2bsn/Higher_Learning_CommissionBacc_Ed_TF.pdf

Levin, J. S. "The Community College as a Baccalaureate-Granting Institution." *The Review of Higher Education,* 2004, 28(1), 1–22.

Levin, J. S., Kater, S., and Wagoner, R. L. *Community College Faculty: At Work in the New Economy.* New York: Palgrave, 2006.

Townsend, B. K. "A Cautionary View." In D. L. Floyd, M. L. Skolnik, and K. P. Walker (eds.), *The Community College Baccalaureate: Emerging Trends and Policy Issues.* Sterling, VA.: Stylus Publishing, 2005.

Wagoner, R. L. "The negotiation of faculty roles and identities: A case study of merged institutions." Paper presented at the meeting of the American Educational Research Association, New Orleans, LA.: April 2011.

Wattenbarger, J. "Colleges Should Stick to What They Do Best." *Community College Week,* 2000, 12(18), 4–5.

RICHARD L. WAGONER *is an assistant professor of higher education and organizational change at the University of California, Los Angeles.*

CARLOS AYON *is a doctoral student of higher education and organizational change at the University of California, Los Angeles.*

This chapter discusses challenges of the next steps along the baccalaureate degree articulation pathway: graduate education. The articulation of community college applied and workforce baccalaureate degrees with university graduate degrees is the next frontier in the community college baccalaureate movement.

Graduate Education Issues and Challenges: Community College Applied and Workforce Baccalaureates

Deborah L. Floyd, Rivka A. Felsher, Linda Catullo

State legislatures and governing bodies in almost twenty states have approved community colleges to offer baccalaureate degrees in areas of high workforce demand fields such as nursing, allied health, teaching, technologies, engineering, and business. These new applied and workforce baccalaureates (AWB) afford students opportunities to earn relevant baccalaureate degree credentials in high demand fields that lead directly to employment. Most AWB degree programs require general education coursework found in university baccalaureate programs, as well as specialized discipline courses. Thus, it is understandable that in addition to the AWB serving as a credential for employment and job advancement, AWB graduates expect their baccalaureate degree to be recognized by universities for admission to post-baccalaureate programs.

The acceptance of community college AWB degrees by university graduate level programs has not been adequately vetted by academics and policymakers. Over the past decade and a half, the primary motivation for offering community college baccalaureate degrees was to fulfill unmet needs in the local workforce and to expand baccalaureate degree access locally. To date, little attention has been given to the next steps for students along a learning pathway that may include graduate education. As the popularity and success of AWBs expands exponentially, graduate articulation

New Directions for Community Colleges, no. 158, Summer 2012 © 2012 Wiley Periodicals, Inc.
Published online in Wiley Online Library (wileyonlinelibrary.com) • DOI: 10.1002/cc.20020

issues must be addressed in the planning, design, and implementation stages of community college baccalaureate (CCB) programs.

Earlier in this monograph Ignash described the articulation of applied associate degrees as a "tangled knot" along pathways to transfer to a baccalaureate education (Ignash, 1997; Ignash & Kotun, 2005). We contend that this "tangled knot" is even more complicated for students who attempt to transfer community college baccalaureate degrees to master's degrees, especially if the issue of graduate education was not addressed early in the curriculum development process. We also believe that articulating these new AWB degrees with university graduate programs presents a new frontier of challenges for higher education leaders.

This chapter focuses on issues, challenges, and questions about transferability of community college applied and workforce baccalaureates (AWB) to graduate-level programs. Our views are grounded in our experience as practitioners and in graduate educators. This new frontier of AWB to graduate degree articulation is worthy of attention by practitioners, researchers, and policymakers.

Challenges in Uncharted Territory

When students graduate from community college AWB programs, what comes next? Certainly, the acceptance and respect of their degree as a valuable credential for employment is a reasonable expectation. But, should AWB graduates also expect that their degrees will be accepted and respected by university graduate programs if they decide to pursue master's degrees?

This new uncharted territory of transitioning from community college awarded AWB degrees to university awarded master's degrees is rich with questions and challenges for practitioners, policy makers, and researchers, such as:

- What are the barriers that AWB graduates face when applying to graduate schools?
- Should AWB degrees be designed to articulate with graduate schools or only developed with the employer in mind?
- Are graduate program articulation agreements necessary or even feasible?
- Will the rigor of an AWB degree be a factor in graduate program admissions, with or without an articulation agreement?
- How can universities partner with colleges to market new articulation agreements and attract more AWB graduates to their master's level programs?
- Will articulated university master's degree programs change and become more relevant to the workforce by strengthening connections with community college AWB degree programs?

NEW DIRECTIONS FOR COMMUNITY COLLEGES • DOI: 10.1002/cc

- Will the success of AWB graduates be determined solely on the value of their credential in the world of work or will the acceptance of the degree by graduate schools be an important expectation?
- Most importantly, what information do we need to ethically provide to prospective students so that they can make informed decisions?

These, and other questions, must be addressed as this community college baccalaureate movement evolves.

Issues for Higher Education Practitioners and Researchers

As more and more students graduate from AWB programs, understandably some graduates will seek opportunities for graduate-level study at some point in their career. Most often, these students will assume that their AWB credits will qualify them for relevant graduate study, but their assumption may be inaccurate. Projecting to the future, Ignash and Kotun's "tangled knot" of CCB delivery goes beyond baccalaureate degree conferral and extends into the realm of university graduate education. We will attempt to address some of the issues, challenges, and questions that are worthy of attention by the higher education community as these new degrees continue to evolve.

Realistic Assessment of Barriers.   University and community college practitioners, policymakers, and researchers need to realistically assess the barriers that will impede the articulation of these new community college AWB degrees with university master's degrees. Historically, articulating community college associate degrees with university baccalaureate degrees has been a recurring challenge that requires local, regional, and state collaboration and partnerships. Working together, community colleges and universities have implemented common course-numbering systems, articulation agreements, and student transfer support systems that have contributed significantly to improving success among associate to baccalaureate degree transfers. These are the types of systems and programs that need to be in place for the articulation of new AWB degrees to university graduate degrees in order to support students who want to pursue graduate study.

The assessment of barriers should be data driven and the process of assessment should be systematically implemented. Data gathered at the assessment stage will help inform decision-making and be useful in shaping articulation agreements, fundraising and resource development, and implementation plans. A systematic assessment process should include the following questions:

- What types of obstacles, if any, are students who have graduated from AWB programs encountering regarding master's degree admission?
- Which courses and which credits will specifically be accepted as prerequisites for a master's program, and which will not?

- What biases, if any, do university faculty have that may be barriers to AWB graduate student success? What plans and programs need to be in place to address the biases that may exist?
- What plans and programs need to be implemented to overcome the barriers to providing AWB programs that will be respected by university graduate schools?

Bachelor's to Master's Articulation.   Because community college AWB degrees are fairly new, it is likely that most community colleges have yet to embrace the meaning of these degrees at the university graduate level much less develop articulation agreements. Community college leaders at institutions offering, or considering offering, AWB degrees should engage university partners and policy makers early in the curriculum process to increase buy-in regarding the acceptance of AWB graduates by university master's programs. Where possible, these efforts should result in formalized articulation agreements that spell out the requirements for successful articulation from community college AWBs to university graduate programs.

Articulation agreements must instruct students on the process of selecting an AWB program that meets their career goals and has the opportunity for graduate study should they later choose to advance their education beyond the baccalaureate. Students will expect to be given accurate information about admissions requirements, college GPA expectations, cost, workforce opportunities, and graduate program opportunities before admission.

In addressing baccalaureate to master's articulation, practitioners, policymakers, and researchers should consider the following questions:

- What are the lessons learned from the successes and failures in associate to baccalaureate degree articulation that will be useful in baccalaureate to master's degree program articulation?
- Can specific universities be identified that are willing to work with the community college to increase the probability that AWB courses and programs will articulate with specific master's degree programs and courses? If so, are these universities willing to work as collaborative partners throughout program planning and implementation?
- What specific graduate programs will the AWB program articulate with? Will the articulation be course-based, program-based, or both?
- What systems and programs need to be implemented to ensure university and community college faculty buy-in from the beginning of the process of considering AWB to master's level articulation?

Ethical Responsibilities for Advising.   It is understandable that today's baccalaureate graduates, regardless of the field, expect their degree to be counted as "real" degrees upon application to graduate schools. But, are they? Many questions surround this issue including those Floyd (2005) posed such as, "What are the ethical and moral responsibilities . . . after completion of the associate degree? Should colleges ensure students understand fully the ramifications of a [community college] baccalaureate . . . including the reality that some universities may not accept these baccalaureates as an entry for graduate studies and beyond?" (p. 44).

College advisors and leaders have an ethical responsibility to ensure that students are accurately and fully informed of the risks associated with these new baccalaureate degrees, especially related to acceptance by graduate schools. Realistic assessments of barriers to transferability must be made and serve as guides for institutional planning, programming, and communications. If the community college has no guarantees that an AWB degree will be recognized by university graduate programs for post-baccalaureate study, students should receive this information early in the advising process so that they may make informed decisions.

Some of the guiding questions practitioners and policymakers should consider about ethical advising include:

- What are our ethical and moral responsibilities for advising and informing students about the value of specific AWB degrees should they wish to pursue post-baccalaureate graduate studies?
- What systems need to be in place for accurately advising students about the projected outcomes of the AWB degree, specifically: entering the world of work; and the potential for admission to graduate school?
- What information will readily be available to students so that they can make informed decisions and when should students be informed?

Defining and Measuring Success.   How will success be defined and measured for community college AWB degree programs and graduates? Will success be measured by the number of highly skills jobs filled locally, the increase in pay for graduates, or an improvement of graduates' quality of life? Will success also be measured by the value of the AWB degree in the eyes of others in higher education, such as university graduate schools? The time has come to recognize that most AWB graduates define their success in two ways: enhanced opportunities for local employment and job advancement; and the acceptance of their credential for appropriate graduate study.

Intentional partnerships should be forged among community colleges, universities, and state systems to track admissions and matriculation data of community college baccalaureate degree students who seek master's degrees and beyond. Most importantly, a conversation about how we will define and measure success needs to be a part of the AWB planning and implementation processes.

Some of the guiding questions practitioners, policymakers, and researchers should consider are:

- How should success be defined and measured? Should it be defined by learning outcomes for AWB graduates, ease of entry and advancement into the workforce, type of employment gained, employment income, community economic development, transfer and articulation to graduate studies, graduate level matriculation processes, quality of life, or other measures?
- What systems and processes need to be in place to determine how AWB student and program success will be defined and measured?
- What data should be collected, when, and by whom, to document and measure student and program outcomes?
- What systems are in place to track and report data about AWB graduates who apply to university graduate programs? If admitted, what systems are in place to track and report matriculation and student outcomes?
- Who should be responsible for tracking and reporting data about outcomes of AWB programs? How will data be utilized for program improvement?

The Next Frontier

We recognize that some critics of community colleges argue that community colleges contribute to social stratification or tracking of students into lower-wage vocational programs as opposed to their university counterparts. However, the new community college AWB degrees counter the perceptions of earlier critics by graduating students who secure higher paying jobs than traditional university baccalaureate degree graduates. In Florida for example, students who graduate with an AWB from a Florida college earn an average entry-level salary of $47,080 while Florida public university graduates earn an average entry-level salary of only $36,552 (The Florida College System, 2010). In reality, the new community college baccalaureate AWB may in fact be an anecdote to social stratification by offering a relevant baccalaureate degree that leads to higher wages and the potential for post-baccalaureate graduate study. But, if graduates of these AWB programs who want access to graduate education are denied entry, then the criticisms of social stratification may be renewed.

Regardless, in our opinion, the next frontier for this movement must include addressing issues of articulating AWB degrees with university graduate degree programs. The entrepreneurial, can-do attitude that has been the trademark of community colleges from their inception is the same attitude that is needed to address these new challenges of graduate articulation of the AWB.

In Conclusion

Community colleges across the United States have a rich history of successfully addressing the challenges of articulating associate degrees to university baccalaureate degrees. The conditions outlined in these successful agreements can and should now be applied to the articulation of the college baccalaureate with the university master's degree. While there may be initial resistance, the importance of these new community college AWB degrees and their potential to lead to graduate study is difficult to deny. The time has come to focus on articulation of community college AWB degrees with appropriate graduate degrees.

In conclusion, higher education practitioners, policy makers, and researchers must realistically assess the barriers to graduate study for AWB graduates and develop systems to remove the barriers. Articulation plans must be in place to "untangle the knot" for graduates of AWB programs who want to pursue university post-baccalaureate studies. Ethical advising processes must be created that provide as much transparency as possible so that potential AWB students can weigh the risks of enrollment. Lastly, scholar-researchers should work with practitioners to define and measure success for AWB degree graduates and programs.

Successfully embracing challenges of graduate articulation is the next challenging frontier for community colleges awarding baccalaureate degrees. This is an exciting time in the history of community colleges because opportunities abound for creatively and persistently embracing the challenges of "what comes next?" for AWB degree graduates.

References

The Florida College System. "The Florida College System Business Plan 2011–2012." Tallahassee, FL: Florida Department of Education, December 2010, at http://www.fldoe.org/cc/pdf/FCS_BusinessPlan.pdf

Floyd, D. L. (2005). "The Community College Baccalaureate in the U.S." In D. L. Floyd, M. L. Skolnik, and K. P. Walker (eds.), *The Community College Baccalaureate: Emerging Trends and Policy Issues.* Sterling, VA.: Stylus Publishing, 2005.

Ignash, J. M. *Results of an Investigation of State Policies for the AAS Degree.* Springfield, Ill.: Illinois Board of Higher Education, 1997. (ED 405 051)

Ignash, J. M., and Kotun, D. "Results of a National Study of Transfer in Occupational Technical Degrees: Policies and Practices." *Journal of Applied Research in the Community Colleges*, 2005, 12(2), 109–120.

DEBORAH L. FLOYD *is a professor and the program leader of higher education leadership at Florida Atlantic University.*

RIVKA A. FELSHER *is a doctoral candidate of higher education leadership at Florida Atlantic University.*

LINDA CATULLO *is director of development at Fredericksburg Academy.*

NEW DIRECTIONS FOR COMMUNITY COLLEGES • DOI: 10.1002/cc

INDEX

A.A.S. degrees. *See* Associate of applied science (A.A.S.)

AASCU. *See* American Association of State Colleges and Universities (AASCU)

AB. *See* Applied baccalaureate degrees (AB)

Abstract conceptualizations, 60

Academic (term), 14

Active experimentation, 60

Advanced Discipline and Management structure, 39

American Community Survey (U.S. Census Bureau), 73–74

American Graduation Initiative (Obama), 73

Andreas, M., 3, 25

Angerilli, N., 59, 63

Apostolides, V., 59

Applied (term), 2, 7; *versus academic*, 14

Applied and workforce baccalaureate programs: and bachelor's to master's articulation, 98; challenge of, to community college mission, 88–89; and challenges in uncharted territory, 96–97; and defining and measuring success, 99–100; and ethical responsibilities for advising, 98–99; graduate education issues and challenges with, 95–101; institutional challenges of, 87–93; and issues for higher education practitioners and researchers, 97–100; models and terminology of, 5–10; next frontier for, 100–101; realistic assessment of barriers of, 97–98; role of faculty in, 91–92; at South Texas College, 47–56; threat of, to community college institutional identity, 89–91

Applied associate degree (A.A.S.): A.A.S.-to-baccalaureate: curriculum, purpose, and target student audience for, 21–23; articulation to and from: challenges and opportunities, 13–23; and defining applied learning, 16–21; and different pathways to baccalaureate, 14–15; purposes of, 14–15

Applied baccalaureate degrees (AB), 5, 15; appeal of, to working adults, 73–84; at

Bellevue College, 19–20; at Columbia Basin College, 17–18; at community and technical colleges, 17–18; comparison of B.A. in business administration and, in applied management, 17; at Evergreen State College, 25–33; models for, 79; need for, in Washington, 26; at Oklahoma State University Institute of Technology, 79–81; and promising practices, 83–84; research on, 75–76; at South Seattle Community College, 81–83; state-by-state inventory of, 76–79; Washington (state) model and programs for, 25–33

"Applied Baccalaureate Developments and Future Implications" (conference; Lumina Foundation), 13

Applied learning, defining, 16–21

Applied science (A.S.) degree, 8

Articulation baccalaureate pathway model, 6, 9

A.S. *See* Applied science (A.S.) degree

Associate of applied science (A.A.S.) degree, 20–21, 75, 81

Associate of applied science-transfer (A.A.S.-T.) degree, 82

Associate of Applied Technology (A.A.T.) degree, 20–21

AWB. *See* Applied and workforce baccalaureate (AWB)

Ayon, C., 3, 87

Bachelor of applied arts and sciences (B.A.A.S.) degrees, 77

Bachelor of applied science (B.A.S.) degree, 8, 15, 16

Bachelor of Applied Science Degree Task Force (Florida Department of Education), 37, 39; Final Report of Activities, 38, 39

Bachelor of applied technology (B.A.T.) degree, 15

Bachelor of general studies (B.G.S.) degree, 8–9

Bachelor of professional studies (B.P.S.) degree, 8–9

Bachelor of technology (B.T.) degree, 79–81

Barnes, T., 14
B.A.S. *See* Bachelor of applied science (B.A.S.) degree
B.A.T. *See* Bachelor of applied technology (B.A.T.) degree
Baylor University, 54
Beckett, D., 65
Bellevue College (Washington): bachelor of applied arts (B.A.A.) in interior design, 19; bachelor of applied science (B.A.S.) in interior design, 28; bachelor of applied science (B.A.S.) in radiation and imaging services, 28; career ladder pathway at, 19–20
Bellevue Community College (Washington), 28
B.G.S. *See* Bachelor of general studies (B.G.S.) degree
Bilsky, J., 3, 35, 40
Boud, D., 60, 67
B.P.S. *See* Bachelor of professional studies (B.P.S.) degree
Bragg, D., 1–3, 7, 9, 25–26, 73–76, 79, 82
Branton, G., 59
Brazosport College (Texas), 50
Breneman, D. W., 74
Brevard State College, 9
Brew, A., 60
Brint, S., 91, 100
B.T. degree. *See* Bachelor of technology (B.T.) degree

CAEL. *See* Council for Adult and Experiential Learning (CAEL)
California, 6, 77
Caloia, D., 45
Campbell, C., 65
Canada, 92
Canadian Council on Learning, 59
Capstone degree, 15; and example of capstone pathway, 16–17
Career ladder applied and workforce baccalaureate, 8, 9, 79
Career ladder pathway, 15; example of, at Bellevue College, 19–20
Carnevale, A. P., 25, 74
Catullo, L., 3, 95
CCB. *See* Community college baccalaureate (CCB)
CCBA. *See* Community College Baccalaureate Association (CCBA)
Central Washington University, 26
Chao, E. L., 74

Chapman, A., 60, 61
Cheek, G. D., 65
Clark, B.B.R., 23
CLAST. *See* Florida College Level Academic Skills Test (CLAST)
CLOs. *See* Course learning outcomes (CLOs)
Closing the Gaps (Texas Higher Education Coordinating Board), 47, 49
Cohen, A. M., 13
Cohen, R., 60
College of Eastern Utah, 92
Co-location model, 6
Columbia Basin College, 16–18, 22; bachelor of applied science (B.A.S.) in management, 28
Community college (term), 10
Community college applied and workforce baccalaureate (AWB), 2; and articulation models, 6; and community college baccalaureate (CCB), 7; description of, 7–8; future of, 9–10; models, 5–10; types of, 8–9; and university centers and concurrent-use models, 6–7
Community College Baccalaureae Association (CCBA), 78
Community college baccalaureate (CCB) degree, 2–3, 5, 7, 9, 78
Concrete experience, 60
Concurrent-use campus models, 6–7
Connecticut, 35
Cooperative education, 59
Council for Adult and Experiential Learning (CAEL), 74
Council for Interior Design Accreditation, 19
Course learning outcomes (CLOs), 61–70
Cutt, J., 59

Davidge-Johnston, N. L., 59
Day, P. A., 60
Daytona State College (Florida), 9
DeRocco, E. S., 74
Discipline Saturation degree structure, 39
Dixie State College, 91
Donald, J., 16
Donohue, M. M., 3, 57, 58

Eakins, P., 65
Eames, C., 59

Eastern Washington University, 26
Eaton, J. S., 87, 88–90
Educational attainment, in ten most populous states, 36 Tab. 1
England-Siegerdt, C., 3, 25
Enterprise model, 6
Evergreen State College, 20–21, 26
Experiential learning theory (Kolb), 59–61

Falconetti, A. M. G., 1, 3, 5, 6, 8
FCS. See Florida College System (FCS)
Felsher, R. A., 1, 3, 5, 95
Findlen, G. L., 14
Finney, J. E., 36
Flick, U., 62
Florida, 2, 3, 6, 8, 78–79, 90–92; academic integrity and regional accreditation in workforce baccalaureate movement in, 43; approval process in workforce baccalaureate movement in, 43; Bachelor of Applied Science Task Force, 37, 38; Commission on Independent Education, 43–44; evolution of workforce baccalaureate degree in, 35–45; growing concern in, 37; and growth over past decade, 40–41; Higher Education Coordinating Council, 44; issues and implications of workforce baccalaureate movement in, 41–45; Legislature, 44; mission of workforce baccalaureate movement in, 42; perspectives on need and demand for workforce baccalaureate in, 35–37; policy and workforce baccalaureate movement in, 42–43; SB 1162, 8, 37; strategic planning and partnerships in, 43–44; 2+2 statewide articulation model, 6, 37
Florida College System (FCS), 6, 8–10, 35–37, 39, 42–44, 100; Community College Program Fund, 44; 2003–2004 headcount and FTE by institution, 40 Tab. 2; 2009–2010 headcount and FTE by institution, 41 Tab. 3
Florida Community College System, 35, 36, 40; Fact Book, 40. See also Florida College System (FCS)
Florida Department of Education, 8, 35, 39–41, 43, 44
Florida State College, Jacksonville, 8
Florida State University System (SUS), 6, 36, 37, 41, 43

Florida Statute 1004.73, 37
Florida Statute 1007.01, 37
Florida Statute 1007.33, 37, 38, 90
Floyd, D. L., 1–3, 5–8, 75, 78, 92, 95, 98–99
Flynn, M. K., 74
Foster School of Business (University of Washington), 16–17

Gajdamaschko, N., 59, 63
Gansneder, B. M., 74
General education (term), 14
General management degree structure, 39
Georgia, 77
Grosjean, G., 58, 59

Hager, P., 65
HECB. See Higher Education and Coordinating Board (HECB; Washington State)
Hidalgo County (Texas), 47
Higher Learning Commission North Central Association of Colleges and Schools, 90
Hispanic students, 3, 47, 52
Holcombe, W., 8
Holdnak, J., 44
Hybrid model, 6–7

Ignash, J. M., 3, 6, 8, 9, 13, 15, 16, 79, 82, 96
Illinois, 6, 77
Illinois Board of Higher Education, 74
Independent Colleges and Universities of Florida, 43–44
Integrated model, 6–7
Interior Design, comparison of B.A. and B.A.A. in, 19
Inverse or upside-down applied and workforce baccalaureate, 8, 9, 79
Inverted baccalaureate degree structure, 15, 39

Jacksonville, Florida, 8
Janus (god of beginnings), 23
Johnson, R. B., 62
Johnston, N., 59, 63

Karabel, J., 100
Kater, S., 89, 92
Kentucky, 6
Kimber, D., 59

King, J., 73
"Knowledge explosion," 36
Kohl, K. J., 74
Kolb, A. Y., 60
Kolb, D. A., 58–64; learning styles of, 60–62
Kolb Learning Style Inventory (LSI), 62
Korean Conflict veterans, 35
Kotun, D., 8, 9, 15, 16, 76, 79, 95

Lake Washington Technical College: bachelor of applied science (B.A.S.) in technology, 28
Lamar University (Texas), 54
Learning to Think (Donald), 16
Levin, J. S., 74, 87–90, 92
Lewin, K., 59–60
LexisNexis, 75
Locke, M. G., 3, 35
Loken, M., 59
Loo, R., 64
Looye, J. W., 59
Lorenzo, A. L., 6, 7
Lumina Foundation for Education, 2, 13, 73–75

Management ladder applied and workforce baccalaureate, 8, 9, 15, 79
Management ladder degrees, 15; example of, 16–18
"Manual arts," 13
Maryland, 22
Massachusetts, 35
Maypole, D. E., 60
McAllen Chamber of Commerce (Texas), 49
McAllen Economic Development Corporation, 49
Mejia, J. E., 3, 47
Michigan, 35, 77
Midland College (Texas), 50
Milam, J. H., 74
Milley, P., 58, 59, 68
Milne, P., 59
Mission Study (Washington State SBCTC), 28–29
Mississippi, 6
Mullin, C., 73

National Center for Education Statistics (NCES; U.S. Department of Education), 36, 73

National Commission on Adult Literacy, 74
National Science Foundation, 79
NCES. See National Center for Education Statistics (NCES; U.S. Department of Education)
Neuhard, I., 3, 35
New Directions for Community Colleges (volume 135), 88
New Jersey, 35
New Mexico State University College of Extended Learning, 9
New York state, 6
Ney, T., 59
Nolan, R. E., 68
North Central Association of Colleges and Schools, 90
Northwest Commission on Colleges and Universities (NWCCU), 27
Northwest Regional Accrediting Association, 17–18
NWCCU. See Northwest Commission on Colleges and Universities (NWCCU)

Obama, B., 25, 73
Ohio, 35
Oklahoma, 6
Oklahoma State University (OSU), 79–80
Oklahoma State University Institute of Technology (OSU-IT), 79–81
Okmulgee, Oklahoma, 79
Olympic College bachelor in science (B.A.S.) in nursing, 28
Ontario, Canada, 3
Ontario college baccalaureate program: and cooperative education, 59; and experiential learning theory, 59–61; findings and analysis regarding, 62–66; literature review for, 58–61; methodology for study on, 61–62; and recommendations for practice, 67–70; research conclusions from study of, 66–67; research questions for study of, 58; work experience component of, 57–70
OSU Institute of Technology Catalog, 81
OSU-IT. See Oklahoma State University Institute of Technology (OSU-IT)

Patridge, Keith, 49
Peninsula College (Washington), 28; Bachelor of applied science (B.A.S.) in management, 28

Perkins, G. R., 6
Perry, Rick, 50
Phillippe, K., 73
Puget Sound (Washington), 82
Pusser, B., 74

Raschick, M., 60
Reed, Shirley, 49
Reflective observation, 60
Richards, Ann, 48
Ricks, F., 59
Rogers, J., 6
Russell, A., 78
Ruud, C. M., 1–3, 7, 9, 25–26, 73–79, 82
Ryder, K. G., 59

Salt Lake Community College (Utah), 91
Saltmarsh, J. A., 59
Sam Huston State University, 54
SBCTC. See Washington State Board for Community and Technical Colleges (SBCTC)
Seattle Central Community College: bachelor of applied science in applied behavioral sciences, 28
Seattle Community College District, 81
Seattle Community Colleges, 81
Seattle-King County, 82–83
Skolnik, M., 1–3, 7, 57
Smith, E. J., 8
Smith, N., 25, 74
Snow College (Utah), 91
South Seattle Community College (SSCC): applied baccalaureate, 81–83; bachelor of sciences (B.A.S.) in hospitality management, 28
South Texas College (STC), 3; applied and workforce baccalaureate at, 47–56; Bachelor of Applied Technology Division, 53; Bachelor of Applied Technology Exit Survey (2009), 52; bachelor of applied technology in computer and information technologies, 51–53; birth of, 50; brief history of, 47–48; challenge and opportunity at, 47–48; Comprehensive Mission of, 56; computer and information technologies at, 51–52; genesis of applied and workforce baccalaureate at, 49; leadership by Texas Legislature at, 49–50; Research and Analytical Services Office, 52, 53; technology management at, 51

South Texas College Bachelor of Applied Technology Exit Survey (2009), 51–52; and employee feedback, 56; employment or status after graduation, 54; key findings of, 54; and Likert scale questions by area of inquiry, 55 Tab. 4; and mentoring, 55; methodology for, 53; purpose of, 53; research questions, 53; and student-faculty interaction, 54–55
South Texas Community College (STCC), 47, 48, 50
Southern Association of Colleges and Schools (SACS), 50; Level II Regional Accreditation, 38, 39, 43
Spaulding, R. S., 25
Sponsorship model, 6–7
SSCC. See South Seattle Community College (SSCC)
St. Petersburg College (Florida), 8, 37, 45
St. Petersburg Junior College (Florida), 37
Stark, J., 59
Starr County (Texas), 47
State college (term), 10
Statistical Abstract (U.S. Census Bureau), 35, 36
STC. See South Texas College (STC)
STEM (science, technology, mathematics, and engineering) programs, 79
Strohl, J., 25, 74

Tennessee, 6
Texas, 6, 35; Education Code, 50; HB 2198, 50; Legislature, 47–48; SB 286, 48–50
Texas A&M University, 54
Texas Higher Education Coordinating Board, 47, 50
Texas State Technical College, Harlingen, McAllen extension center, 47–48
Tomsho, R., 36
Townsend, B. K., 6, 7, 9, 14, 25–26, 74, 75_, 76, 82, 88, 90
Travis, S., 36–37
Tulsa, Oklahoma, 79
Turner, S. E., 74
2008 Strategic Master Plan for Higher Education in Washington (Washington State HECB), 28–29

University center baccalaureate pathway model, 6–7, 9

University extension baccalaureate pathway model, 6–7, 9
University of Central Florida, 36–37
University of Florida, 36–37
University of North Florida, 36–37
University of South Florida, 36–37
University of Texas, 54
University of Washington, 17, 18, 81–82
University of West Florida (UWF). *See* Florida College Level Academic Skills Test (CLAST)
University of Wisconsin System, 77
Upside down baccalaureate degree, 15; comparison of, with B.A. in general studies degree pathways, 21; example of pathway of, at Evergreen State College, 20–21
U.S. Census Bureau, 35, 36, 73–74
U.S. Department of Education, 36
Utah, 6, 91, 92
Utah State University Eastern, 91, 92
Utah Valley University, 91

Van Gyn, G. H., 59, 68
Vince, R., 60
Virginia, 6
Virtual model, 6–7

Wagoner, R. L., 3, 87, 89_, 92
Walker, D., 60, 67
Walker, K. P., 1–2, 7, 8, 78
Washington (state), 3, 6, 78–79, 82; applied baccalaureate degrees at community and technical colleges, 25–33; approving pilot programs in, 27–28; current approval process and criteria in, 29–30; HB 1794, 26–27; lessons learned for institutions from, 31–32; lessons learned for policymakers from, 30–31; making case for additional degree programs in, 28–29; need for applied baccalaureate degrees in, 26; response of legislature in, 26–27; Senate Substitute Bill 6355, 29
Washington Higher Education Coordinating Board (HECB), 23, 25–32, 82; Education Committee, 30
Washington State Board for Community and Technical Colleges (SBCTC), 22–23, 26–32
Washington State University, 81–82; Department of Interior Design, 19
Wattenbarger, James, 35, 87, 88, 90
Weber State University (Utah), 91
Weisz, M., 59
Wellman, J. V., 6
Western Washington University, College of Humanities and Social Sciences, 20–21
Windham, P., 6
Wisconsin, 6, 14
Workforce (term), 2
Workforce baccalaureate, 5
Workforce Training and Education Coordinating Board (WTECB), 27, 29
Working adults, appeal of applied baccalaureates to, 73–84
World War II veterans, 35
WTECB. *See* Workforce Training and Education Coordinating Board (WTECB)